Anonymous

Art Needlework

A complete manual of embroidery in silks and crewels, with full

instructions as to stitches, materials, and implements. Containing also a

large number of original designs and a handsome coloured design for

crewel work

Anonymous

Art Needlework

A complete manual of embroidery in silks and crewels, with full instructions as to stitches, materials, and implements. Containing also a large number of original designs and a handsome coloured design for crewel work

ISBN/EAN: 9783337386627

Printed in Europe, USA, Canada, Australia, Japan

Cover: Foto ©Thomas Meinert / pixelio.de

More available books at **www.hansebooks.com**

ART NEEDLEWORK.

A COMPLETE MANUAL OF

EMBROIDERY IN SILKS AND CREWELS,

WITH FULL INSTRUCTIONS AS TO

STITCHES, MATERIALS, AND IMPLEMENTS.

CONTAINING ALSO

A LARGE NUMBER OF ORIGINAL DESIGNS

AND

A Handsome Coloured Design for Crewel Work.

LONDON:

WARD, LOCK, AND CO., WARWICK HOUSE,

SALISBURY SQUARE, E.C.

NEW YORK: 10, BOND STREET.

THE WILD FLOWER DESIGN FOR EMBROIDERY IN CREWELS, SIZE 6.
SUITABLE FOR CURTAINS AND CHAIR-BACKS AFTERNOON TEA-CLOTHS SIDE-BOARD COVERS, PIN CUSHIONS &C.

PREFACE.

—✕—

THE popularity of that kind of Embroidery popularly known as "Art Needlework" increases with every year, and the rage for Crewels is likely to last for a very long time. The present volume has been prepared with a view to supplying practical instructions so clearly given as to obviate the necessity for attending a school of Art Needlework. The stitches are fully described and elucidated by diagrams. The various modes of transferring designs from paper to material are clearly explained, and every information is given as to materials, implements, and mode of working that can assist the learner. At the same time, the more experienced worker will find fresh designs and fresh ideas in the following pages. The remarks on colour are calculated to be of use both to novice and proficient, while the accuracy of the drawings of flowers and leaves may thoroughly be depended upon as true to nature. We have, in fact, endeavoured to render the work so complete as to make it an indispensable adjunct of the work-table.

CONTENTS.

LIST OF ILLUSTRATIONS.

ART NEEDLEWORK.

CHAPTER I.

THE recent fashion for "art needlework" has given an impetus to one of the most ancient of feminine occupations. From the days when the Israelitish women wove and decorated hangings for the tabernacle, and Grecian princesses did not disdain to embroider garments—from the very dawn of history down to the present time, needlework has been a woman's special and favourite occupation. Beautiful specimens of the art have come down to us, as the present exhibition of ancient needlework exhibited at South Kensington shows. The era of Berlin wool work has happily passed away, and needlework is again taking its place among the ornamental arts. Some years ago it was rather the fashion to decry this formerly popular accomplishment, advocates of the "higher education" for women openly stating that they trusted a day was coming when the needle would no longer be a familiar implement in female fingers. Probably this was a reaction from the excessive importance attached to needlework in the last century, when it was held up as an ideal epitaph, "She died at a good old age, having wrought out the whole Bible in tapestry." There is said to be an inscription on a tomb of the eighteenth century which concludes, "She excelled in needlework, she painted in water-colour—of such is the kingdom of heaven."

Addison, in the *Spectator*, playfully rebukes this excessive devotion to the work of the fingers alone by the story of some young ladies educated by a "notable" mother, whose whole time is so devoted to working "sets of hangings" and cushions that they have never learnt to read or write. Yet even Addison waxes eloquent in praise of "the delightful art of needlework," and devotes a whole number of his periodical to its praise.

If once too highly valued, needlework has certainly been unjustly depreciated. Queen Elizabeth and Mary Queen of Scots were undeniably highly-educated and accomplished women, but the mastery of Greek and Latin did not prevent both finding time to acquire the humbler art of needlework. Beautiful specimens of their handiwork still exist, and the latter queen found her needle the best friend of her dreary hours of captivity. The long years spent in prison would have been intolerable save for the solace found in this amusement, and her correspondence is full of allusions to various purchases of materials for work, and gifts of specimens of her skill. From the earliest days needlework was considered a fitting accomplishment for a princess, and the higher the rank the more the lady was expected to excel in this art. Many a piece of work has become historical. Penelope's famous web has been sung by Homer. Queen Matilda has left a history of the Norman Conquest in the Bayeux tapestry. Englishwomen were celebrated as embroideresses long before William landed at Hastings, the "opus Anglicanus" being sought for ecclesiastical vestments all over the continent. When we see specimens of work of the twelfth century yet extant in good preservation it speaks well for the skill of the worker and the goodness of the materials employed.

The excellence of these latter is one of the first ideas that occur in surveying the collection of ancient needlework at Kensington. Silks of the sixteenth and seventeenth centuries appear as bright as if worked yesterday. After all, although much time was doubtless employed in executing some of the elaborate counterpanes and curtains displayed there, the patient embroideress left a lasting and beautiful possession to her descendants. Many of the old workers handled their needle as an artist does his pencil, and left as pleasing (and almost as lasting) results of their labours. There is a satin dress exhibited at Kensington, worked at an orphanage in the eighteenth century, which might fairly compete for a prize in any exhibition of drawings of flowers. Scattered at intervals over the satin are tiny, exquisitely-worked sprays of flowers, pansies, violets, jessamines, so delicately coloured, so deftly shaded, that they must certainly have been copied from nature by an artist who preferred to work with a needle instead of a paint-brush. One can only wonder at any one liking to *wear*, and risk injuring, so beautiful a specimen of artistic toil. All embroideresses of the same date were not equally tasteful, as an elaborately-worked costume in the next case shows. Much patient labour has been expended on this dress, but the pattern includes, among other things, cottages with smoke issuing from the chimneys, ruined castles, and various other equally clumsy designs, reminding one of the lady of the last century, who, by way of a novelty, ordered a petticoat embroidered with the seven orders of architecture. Ancient needlework was far more the actual product of the worker than modern embroideries generally are. Nearly every lady invented and designed her own patterns, and the work thus took the impress of the worker's individuality. Hence we find such diversity in the specimens that have come down to us. Nearly all are equally well executed, as far as the mechanical art of stitchery is concerned, but there is wide diversity in the effect produced. Some of the dresses and hangings would be beautiful as pictures; some are so hideous that one marvels that any one could work patiently on, month after month, to perpetuate such monstrosities. Perhaps the reward was in the doing; the quiet, regular employment may have cheered many a dull hour, and eased many a heart-ache. Many a woman has found refuge from her troubles in needlework, although some now appear to despise the art. Mrs. Delany, one of the best workers of the eighteenth century, found amusement in diversion in her needle during the dreary years of the loveless marriage into which her friends had forced her. Her interesting "Letters" are a perfect chronicle of needlework, of which she was so indefatigable a professor, and the art stood her in good stead even into old age. As we have said, Mary Queen of Scots lightened her imprisonment with the labours of her needle; and another equally unfortunate but more blameless Queen—poor Marie Antoinette—whiled away the dreary hours of incarceration in the temple by similar means. It is recorded that she, Madame Elizabeth, and the young princess regularly devoted certain hours of the day to needlework.

It seems strange to add the name of an emphatically strong-minded woman to the list of celebrated workers. Yet Harriet Martineau was an adept with her needle, and had indeed supported herself by her beautiful fancy work, long before her books could find a publisher. To the end of her life she was a skilful needlewoman, and took pleasure in the exercise of her skill. It seems a pity that needlework should ever become a "lost art." The hideous Berlin wool-work, and kindred tasteless specimens of misdirected labour, are indeed worthily consigned to oblivion; but in educating our girls' brains, it seems a pity to totally neglect the training of their fingers. A visit to Kensington will show that for decorative purposes a needle is no despicable instrument. The sewing-machine may have swept away the deft "plain workers'" occupation, as the steam spinning-machines have abolished the distaff and spinning-wheel; but in these days of elaborate domestic ornamentation there is ample scope for the exercise of nimble fingers and tasteful inventions. Without encroaching on the time required for a high-class education, girls might learn the art practised by their ancestresses in all ages, an art not to be despised in days of sickness or trouble, when even the favourite book fails to fix the wearied attention, and the sad heart cannot rouse itself to take pleasure in the accustomed study. Then the mechanical occupation of the fingers becomes a valuable resource. Even the old Norse kings recognised the good of some such amusement, for though they left the labours of the loom and the needle to their wives, they did not despise

> "Twisting of collars their dogs for to hold,
> And combing the mane of their coursers bold."

As Addison remarks, "These hours thrown away in dress, play, and visits would suffice to work chairs and beds for the whole family." At least, time so employed would leave a pleasing memorial in the shape of ornamental objects behind it. We believe that the terrible things entitled "fancy work" some years ago served to bring ornamental needlework altogether into disfavour. Alum baskets, cardboard constructions, wax flowers—would any of these serve to delight future (or present) generations? Loan exhibitions of needlework preach the doctrine of the "survival of the fittest." The fair dame of Henry or Elizabeth's court has long passed away, but her beautiful handiwork remains still fresh and untarnished, ornamental in the nineteenth century as in the sixteenth. Some of the patient workers of samplers appear to have realised the enduring quality of their handiwork and secured their names a temporary fame by adding them at the foot. One grateful pupil commemorates that of her teacher also, "Instructed by Alice Underwood."

Few people, in these days of taste and bustle, would have patience to undertake the elaborate designs of our ancestresses, when several generations toiled at a suite of tapestry—the daughter taking up the needle as the mother laid it down, and the great-grandchild,

1.—WORK-BASKET.

2.—HOP-LEAF.

3.—EMBROIDERY FOR WORK-BASKET No. 1.

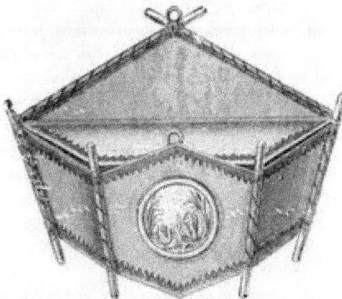

4.—WASTE-PAPER BASKET.

5.—EMBROIDERY FOR No. 4.

6,—Work-Basket (Open).

7.—Embroidery for No. 8.

8.—Penwiper.

9.—Embroidered Sachet.

10.—Work-Basket (Shut).

perhaps, completing the task. But in those times all went gradually. Builders of cathedrals were content to lay out a vast plan, and wait for successive ages to complete the mighty pile. Still much beautiful needlework may be executed in fairly brief space, and the present revival of a taste for it ought to rejoice lovers of domestic decoration. Skill in needlework is a desirable accomplishment for every woman, and in some cases it may prove actually profitable (as Harriet Martineau found it), in others it may serve, like the poet's rhyme,

> " The mechanic exercise
> Like dull narcotics numbing pain."

Lady Jane Grey, who was mistress of eight languages, and was looked upon as quite a prodigy by all learned men of her day, was as skilful with her needle as she was learned in mind. Sir Thomas Challoner, who wrote a Latin poem in her praise, in 1579, specially records that,

> "Inimitably fine
> Her needle wrought."

With such an example, there is little fear that the revival of a taste for needlework need prove an obstruction to the higher education of women.

Once more the tapestry-work of our grandmothers has come into vogue, and our leisure hours are busied with tracing, designing, and crewel-work. The crewel embroidery of to-day is as superior to the old-fashioned Berlin wool-work as it is possible to conceive. In the one Nature is the model, in the other—anything. As long as one can follow a pattern—that is to say, count the stitches and match the wools required—one can do Berlin wool-work. In crewel-work or art embroidery the worker requires to be possessed of some taste, ingenuity, and a slight knowledge of drawing. The wool used in this embroidery may be purchased in almost any shade. To such a charming extent is this carried that a freshly-plucked flower may be faithfully copied in its every gradation of colour—a boon that certainly never belonged to Berlin wool-work. For some time past a very superficial sort of attention has been given to the needle and its productions. This is, no doubt, owing mainly to the advent of the sewing-machines.

Let it not be supposed for one moment that we would say one word against these useful little articles. On the contrary, we are obliged to acknowledge with hundreds of English-women the great boon they have been to us, and are; but, on the other hand, they have encouraged—amongst our young girls especially—an indolence with regard to plain sewing that is not likely to benefit our fancy works.

To gain a thorough proficiency with the needle it is necessary first to practise plain sewing, and then art and fancy needlework follow, just as in drawing one first learns to make straight lines, ovals, curves, &c., before venturing on the shading and perspective which make the picture itself.

Embroidery is one of the oldest of the arts. We read of it in the Bible as used and worn by the ancients. In the ornamentation of the ark we read that the veil of the ark was adorned with "cunning work," and the priestly robes of Aaron and his two sons were richly embroidered. "Upon the hems pomegranates of blue and purple, scarlet and twined linen."

"And they made bells of fine gold, and put the bells between the pomegranates on the hem of the robe."

Embroidery was much used in Egypt for dresses and furniture. It is said that even the sails of the slave-ships were worked upon. The gods of Egypt had their vestments richly

11.—EMBROIDERY FOR SACHET NO. 9.

embroidered, and had many "changes," according to the different seasons. It was from the Egyptians that the Israelites gained their knowledge of embroidery, which knowledge was of material help to them in building and decorating the ark.

Syria was famous for the richness of her embroidery, as were also Tyre, Asshur, Dedan, Sheba, Chilmal, &c. The Greeks especially were great lovers of all kinds of ornamentation, and used much embroidery in their dress and religious ceremonies. In nearly every house there was a "studio" set apart for weaving and embroidery. No pains were spared to make the work perfect. We should do well to copy them in this particular. The Romans, too, ever luxurious in their tastes, indulged largely in embroidery and fancy stuffs, though, unlike the industrious Greeks, they imported most of it from the East.

Embroidery flourished mostly in England about the time of the Middle Ages. In the time of the Saxons it reached a very high perfection, and as the race diminished so in proportion did the artistic tendencies of the people. The embroidery of this time was called "opus Anglicanum," and was mostly done by religious men and women in the convents and abbeys. In history some allusions are made which show to what extent the trade in embroidery was carried on. The names of some of the principal artists are given us. In the reign of Edward the Third it is recorded that payment was made to John de Colonia for two vests of green velvet embroidered with gold, a white robe worked with pearls, and a robe of velvet embroidered with gold. Also to William Courtenay for a royal robe worked with pelicans, images, and tabernacles in gold. Women and men both made this art a perfect business, and it proved a remunerative one too. The great ladies who had little else to do perfected themselves in nearly every branch of fancy work, often making extensive offers to the Church.

Now the "rage" for embroidery is once more apparent among us, we shall, no doubt, find hidden away in our lumber-rooms and wardrobes specimens of samplers, &c., worked by fingers long since cunningless. Our crewel-stitch will be found very similar and well adapted for copying them. There is such a deliciously antique look about a room in which the furniture or curtains are handsomely worked, that our readers, if not possessed of ample means, by good taste and industry may have at least one *æsthetic* room in their house.

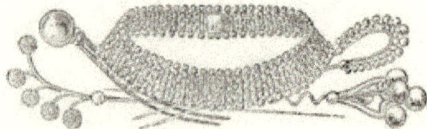

CHAPTER II.

MATERIALS FOR ART NEEDLEWORK.

MATERIALS that may be worked upon are so numerous and varied that it hardly seems like exaggeration to say that almost any material may be embroidered upon, from linen, serge, &c., to the richest satin and velvet. Towelling of a loose texture is a capital material to begin upon. It is not difficult to work, and as it is very cheap the matter is not very great if it gets spoiled in the first attempt. Children should also be given it to learn upon. It makes very good antimacassars, table and toilet mats, d'oyleys, &c.

"Crash" is as much used as any material for crewel-work, and is very useful for small items, such as mats, &c., though we should certainly not recommend it for curtains or portières.

Pretty tea-cloths may be made from white linen. This can be obtained of a very good width, and looks really well, especially if the design be a close one and not too small. Extra fine linen is frequently used for coloured silk embroidery, and looks well if nearly the whole surface has to be covered.

Twilled linen, which is very stout in make, is much used for borderings. The width of this material is so narrow that this is about the only use it may be put to.

Cotton materials, such as workhouse sheeting, muslin, twill cotton, &c., are much used for embroidery. Children's dresses of workhouse sheeting have a very good appearance when worked with crewel wool, and are strong and useful, with the additional merits of cheapness and washing well.

Muslin—always a pretty material—looks charming when embroidered with silk or crewels. Scarves, aprons, fichus, &c., of this material make elegant little additions to our toilet, and only need a minimum of skill and industry to effect. India muslin, if worked in gold and floss silk, looks quite Oriental, and could not be purchased for a light sum.

Twill cotton is a very strong material, and mostly used for covering furniture. This may be obtained in several shades. When a suite of furniture is faded or in any way dilapidated and unsightly it is possible to renovate it by covering the chairs, lounges, ottomans, &c., with this material well worked with crewels, while the curtains, hangings, and portière should match in pattern.

Among the woollen materials serges, cloths, merinos, and cashmere take a prominent part. These may all be obtained in a charming diversity of shades and colours, and may be worked either in silks or crewels.

Imagine a robe of pale pink cashmere worked with ruddy autumn leaves, touched here and there with yellow and silver, and interspersed with small sprays of white wood-violets and leaves. This, if worn by a brunette, would produce about as charming an effect as is possible. Such a costume would be suitable for a garden party or picnic. The hat to match should be large, so as to shade the face, and lined with pale pink satin, edged with narrow cream lace. The pale pink satin drapery round the crown should be worked similarly to the dress, and fastened off at the side with a bunch of white violets and autumn leaves. This drapery should also be edged with narrow cream lace.

Serge is a capital foundation for embroidery. The ribbed surface takes the work well, and shows it to its fullest advantage. Cloth can also be used for the same purpose, though in this the rougher pile is a rather better foundation than the more glossy smooth surface of the finer cloths. It frequently happens that the harsher materials are better to work upon than the thicker, softer stuffs.

Every kind of silk may be embroidered, from the thinnest sarcenet to the richest grosgrain silk.

Of all materials used for embroidery there is none to be compared with satin for beauty and softness. The shimmering light upon its surface softens the harshest shades and harmonises the most opposite colours. To the complexion it is one of the most becoming of materials. We should strongly recommend ladies to patronise it freely.

Blue is not as a rule a satisfactory colour to use as a foundation for embroidery; it is too harsh and cold; but in satin and serge any colour may be used, as the play of light and shade on the surface of the one and the hairy, ribbed surface of the other carry off the usually crude effect caused by a large expanse of blue.

Velvet is a good deal used for crewel-work, both in cotton and silk. There is a ribbed velveteen which makes a good foundation for crewel-work, and well adapted for mantel-hangings and portières. Utrecht velvet may be used for the same purposes. The most expensive velvet— viz., that in which the pile is the shortest—is best adapted for crewel-work. This material, together with thick rep silks, should always form the foundations for ecclesiastical embroidery. The embroidery itself is principally executed in crewels, silks, chenille, and plush. Crewel wool is a kind of worsted very different to Berlin wool in texture and colour. It is possible to obtain a colour of great brilliancy without a touch of harshness, and there is so great a variety in the tints and shades that in using this wool it is possible to make one's design as artistic in its "shadings" as a painting. Crewel wool is much thinner than Berlin wool, being made with two plies only, the loose twist of which in working causes it to form lines like those of a copperplate engraving.

The silks used in the embroidery come under the head of Dacca, Mitorse, filoselle, floss, and purse silks. Sewing silks when thick and soft may also be used; this kind is usually sold in skeins.

Filoselle is the raw material from which spun silk is made; it is more easy to work with

12.—EMBROIDERY FOR WORK-BASKET Nos. 6 & 10.

than floss, and on that account more popular. The French call it *bourre de soie*. It is made from those cocoons of silk from which the moths have been permitted to emerge, and as these are known by the name of "waste cocoons," it is cheap as well as durable.

Mitorse is much used by the Japanese in those exquisite double embroideries executed by them, but as we English are less skilled in the use of our needle it would be better to keep to the Berlin silk, which makes an excellent substitute, and does not require so much care in handling.

Floss is the most difficult silk to work with, Dacca being more universally used on account of the readiness with which it can be split into fragments.

Gold and silver silks are mostly used for church purposes at present, though there is every probability of our ultimately using them in our toilets.

Chenille used in combination with silk was formerly much in vogue for embroidering the most costly stuffs. It is not so frequently used now, though there seems a hint of this pretty material coming up again.

Embroidery over cardboard is very little used except for church purposes, though it is occasionally used in the home for working devices or monograms upon mantel valances or curtains.

The design should first be drawn upon the cardboard in pencil, and then cut out with a sharp penknife or scissors. Then place it on the material, and secure it with strong thread. There is a thin kind of mounting-board which is the best for this purpose.

CHAPTER III.

IMPLEMENTS.

THE implements used in Art Needlework are not many in number, but are none the less important on that account. Needles, a frame, a stiletto, and a piercer comprise the most-needed tools; nor must we forget to mention the useful paste or gum.

The needles should be either the ordinary round-eyed needles or the long-eyed embroidery needles. This depends mostly upon the material they are used for, and must be left to the discretion of the worker. Never allow your needle to be too thick, nor the eye of insufficient size to take the wool easily, or in drawing it backwards and forwards you will find your wool rendered thin and poor. If a needle is too short it requires to be dragged through the stuff, which process can hardly be said to improve its general appearance, besides trying the patience of the worker and giving her a great deal of unnecessary trouble. Therefore take care that your needle be neither too thick nor too thin, too long nor too short, and let the eye be in every way *sans reproche*.

The next article in our category is a frame; the ordinary four-piece frame used in embroidery is too well known to need description. The tambour-frame, consisting of two hoops fitted closely the one within the other, is the more suitable for dresses or any other large pieces of work. Some people imagine that working at a frame is more tedious than otherwise; this is in most cases a mistake, for as the frame effectually holds the work, it relieves the worker, gives her more scope for her postures, proves an enemy to back-ache, leaves both hands at liberty, keeps the work free from puckers, and, if anything, is easier to work with than without.

The use of the stiletto is to make the holes through which the cord-edging has to be taken in embroidering a pattern. The holes should never be made too large, and the whole of this process effected with the utmost neatness and precision.

The piercer is invaluable for laying the threads in gold or silver embroidery, and in raising the work either in crewels or silk. In church embroidery it is used for working silk over cardboard. This little instrument is made of steel, which is round and pointed at one end, resembling a stiletto, and flat at the other.

13.—WORK-BOX.

14.—DETAIL OF WORK-BOX.

15.—EMBROIDERY FOR WORK-BASKET No. 17.

Now a word for the paste or gum, which, perhaps, my readers have been wondering about, as to its connection with Art Needlework. When the material used for the foundation of the embroidery is thin, it is customary to line it with linen or paper by smearing it lightly with paste or gum and pressing it down upon the material. This makes it more substantial and easy to work upon, besides preventing its getting dragged or torn.

16.—TOILET-CUSHION.

17.—WORK-BASKET. FOR DETAIL SEE No. 15.

18.—EMBROIDERY FOR ARM-CHAIR No. 10.

A frame is positively necessary when the embroidery is executed over cardboard with floss silk. The process is as follows:—A strip of strong linen or tape should be stitched along the woof ends of the material, which must then be sewn firmly with strong thread to the webbing on the frame. It is better to use the thread double for this purpose. When this has been done the laths of the frame are to be slipped through the mortice-holes of the other pieces, and the pegs fastened in. The strain should be increased gradually and cautiously till the tension appears sufficient. The woof ends must now be braced to the side-pieces with fine twine. A packing-needle threaded with twine must be drawn through the upper right-hand corner of the tape or linen, and the end tied most securely. The twine must be sewn over the lath till the lower corner is reached, knotted securely, and cut off; the other side must be done in the same manner.

When the material is larger than the frame it may be sewn on to the bars and rolled round one of them with tissue-paper and wadding between, to prevent the creasing of it.

15.—MUSIC-STAND. FOR DETAIL SEE No. 11.

When the portion in the frame is finished it is rolled round the opposite bar, and so on till the work is finished. Or it may be managed in this way, if the stuff to be wrought upon be precious:—Brace a piece of fine holland in the frame, and then carefully place a portion of the velvet or satin in the holland, and tack it down with small stitches and fine thread. When this piece of the work is finished, take it out, put in fresh holland, and spread another portion of material. In this way large surfaces may be covered very easily and well. A large frame adds greatly to the fatigue of the worker, and is really very seldom necessary.

Every worker must be careful to observe that her hands are not only scrupulously clean, but also perfectly smooth. A roughened forefinger will be found to tease and roughen the wool, and it should be smoothed with pumice-stone before commencing operations.

The dress must next engage the attention, and pendants of all kinds, bangles, rings, &c., with which we are so fond of adorning ourselves, be rigorously excluded. These are apt to catch in the work, and frequently occasion serious mishaps. In the winter the hands should be washed in oatmeal and carefully dried, so that no erasure of the skin ensues. In the summer it would be well to wash them often in warm water, so as to prevent their getting moist or damp, especially if engaged in delicate work.

If the dress of the worker be not perfectly clean and fresh, a bibbed apron and sleevelets will be found to keep all pure from dust, and should be kept as part of the worker's paraphernalia. If the apron is made with large pockets, they will be found useful to hold an ample supply of materials, or even to hold one end of the stuff if the piece of work engaged upon be large. This prevents the weight of the material from proving a fatigue, as it affords an effectual support to it and leaves the hands and arms unburdened. Thus attired the worker will not be particularly vain of her reflection, though we should imagine an anxious

12.—Embroidered Chair. For Detail see No. 13.

worker to be perfectly willing to sacrifice small personalities for the sake of the spotlessness of her work. Every kind of work needs care and delicate handling; even the coarsest towelling will show the difference between careless and dainty manipulation.

Paste—every one can make paste, you will say. This, however, is not the case, and as a few of my readers may not know the recipe, we give it here:—Mix some flour and water in a saucepan, add a pinch of resin or alum to every handful of flour. When you have mixed it smoothly, put it on the fire and stir till quite thick. A wooden spoon is the best for this purpose.

Paste should not be kept more than a week. In spreading it upon the back of a material it is better to use the fingers rather than a brush, in order that no little lumps get overlooked. When the material is especially thin, like sarcenet for instance, it may be first lined and then backed with paper. It is so much easier to work through a material of some stability than through a flimsy one, that this little trouble at the outset saves a deal of time afterwards. The paste should be allowed to dry thoroughly before the embroideress sets to work. When a material is thus substantially lined the use of a frame becomes essential.

Embroidery is occasionally executed first upon linen, and afterwards applied to more costly stuffs. When this is done, the design should first be worked and then be backed by paper. When it is done it should be removed from the frame and cut round with a pair of sharp scissors, leaving a narrow edging of the linen round the embroidered part. By means of this little edging the embroidery is applied to the velvet and tacked on strongly with tiny stitches. A gold or silver cord run on with sewing silk will hide the bare edge of the design and add a richness to the effect. A handsome piece of embroidered work will often outlive the material surrounding it, and in this case it may, of course, be transferred if necessary to half-a-dozen materials in succession.

When a piece of work is finished our paste is brought into requisition to smear over the back, after the linings have been removed. This prevents the ends and fastenings of the silk or wool from coming undone, and effectually keeps the whole "tidy."

Collar, Cuff, and Pocket of Dress, with Cutwork Embroidery of Violets, Leaves, and Marsh **Mallow**.

CHAPTER IV.

TRACING AND TRANSFERRING.

THIS part of the programme is a somewhat wearisome one, and requires careful consideration. To those ladies whose knowledge of drawing enables them at once to draw their designs upon the material we offer our sincere congratulations that they are thus enabled to escape a tedious process—while to those workers who lack the courage so to do, or who really cannot draw accurately, we tender this chapter of instructions.

To these last-named, however, we must just give a word of advice and encouragement. Flowers, ferns, leaves, &c., require little exactitude of form and size, and a lady with little or no talent may easily effect them with the barest knowledge of drawing. And as a greater freedom of effect is certainly gained by drawing one's design straight off upon the material, we should advise every worker to—at least—*attempt* it for herself.

In a set design, however, such as an ornamental scroll, the case is different, and even a skilful draughtswoman might lack the courage to effect this without help, especially if the material worked upon be a costly one. For such alternatives, therefore, we will give instructions for tracing and transferring.

The design should first be traced upon cartridge or drawing-paper by holding the design up to the glass of a window and tracing it upon the drawing-paper by means of a pencil or pen.

Another way is to place tissue-paper above the design and trace it through, then to transfer it to the drawing-paper by means of transfer-paper placed between the two. The design in this case should be carefully gone over with an ivory style. The design upon the drawing or cartridge paper should now be pricked carefully and evenly with a pin or steel point. The next move is to lay the pricked design on the cartridge-paper upon the material and rub pounce or pouncing-powder through the holes. When this is done and the cartridge-paper has been removed the material will be found covered with little dots in the shape of the

design. The pounce should be rubbed on with a little brush, or, if the worker doesn't object
to soil her hands, the finger is not at all a bad substitute.   When the halves or four quarters

51.—EMBROIDERY MUSIC-STAND FOR No. 19.

of a design correspond with each other, the quickest and most accurate mode of drawing is
to fold the paper into two or four divisions and draw upon the upper side only.   The holes

may then be pricked through all four divisions at once, and by this means a much more correct pattern is obtained than if the whole were gone over separately.

"Bank post" paper is cheaper and thinner than cartridge-paper, which last is too thick to fold in this manner, so we should recommend the former to our readers.

A very good pounce can be made from pulverised pipeclay, or powder-blue, pipeclay, and charcoal make a capital dark pounce if the material to be traced upon be a light one.

In thus pouncing the design great care must be taken to place it exactly in the centre of the material so that no second trial is needed. For this reason it is better to keep the whole in its place by means of weights. A second trial usually makes the dotted impression blurred and indistinct.

When the pricked outline has been removed the design must be gone over upon the material with paint or Indian ink. This last should be always used in the case of white linen, and can best be put on with a pen. For painting the outline a stiff sable is the best kind of brush. Make each sweep of the brush as free and bold as possible, or the design will be stiff and feeble, and the embroidery consequently an inferior performance. If in painting upon outline a mistake should occur—and we all know how easily that happens—the easiest way to remove the paint is to put a little turpentine into a saucer, and with a piece of rag rub the material briskly; this will quite remove all traces of the paint. We should, however, advise all workers to be cautious in so doing, and by no means to do it more than once. Do not use pouncing powder with hairy materials such as serge or woollen goods; white oil paint will be found suitable for these. The quickest way of all to obtain a pattern is to tack it to the material and follow the outline with stitches, and then to carefully tear away the pattern; this, however, ruins the design, which would otherwise perhaps come in again for a similar matter.

There is a tracing apparatus invented by Mr. Francis, 16, Hanway-street, Tottenham-court-road, which is, I believe, a very excellent substitute for the usual mode of tracing and transfer. A piece of prepared cloth is placed between the material and the paper pattern and the design traced over with a hard lead pencil supplied for the purpose. When this has been done, and the pattern and cloth have been removed, the design will be found perfectly traced. This saves all the trouble of pouncing. The cloth is prepared in two colours, white and blue. The blue is suitable for light materials, the white for dark. A piece of cloth of each colour, and blue and white pencils, together with full directions for use, are supplied for 2s. 6d. by the inventor. A lady who gives much time to embroidery will do well to devote a month, or even two, to learning drawing. It is an excellent thing to be able to design as well as draw one's patterns, while a very fascinating amusement is to copy a bunch of natural flowers, which may afterwards be "painted in worsted." Of course this requires a knowledge of drawing and some ingenuity of imagination. There are some people who would never have a real "taste" for drawing if they were to learn for a dozen years, and to these especially we give the above instructions for tracing and transferring.

CHAPTER V.

STITCHES AND MODE OF WORKING.

ONE of the oldest and most fascinating of stitches is the crewel or long stitch once so fashionable among our grandmothers for tapestry-work, and now revived again among us, we hope, in its fullest perfection. It is decidedly the least mechanical of all the stitches used in fancy work, and much discretion in its practice is left to the worker. For this reason it has a peculiar charm for most workers, while one who is skilful will know just how to adapt it to the particular design she is engaged upon, and thus obtain a better effect than if a settled rule only were applicable to it.

DIAGRAM 1.—CREWEL STITCH.

DIAGRAM 2.—WORKING AN OUTLINE.

DIAGRAM 3.—WORKING AN OUTLINE.

DIAGRAM 4.—SHADING.

The following are the instructions for the popular "long stitch:"—

A knot being made in the worsted it is brought from the under side of the cloth or linen to the surface, then the needle is passed back again from the upper side at about a quarter of an inch distance, more or less. It is again brought up at about half-way from the first point and carried on at about as far beyond the second. (See Diagram 1.)

The length of the stitches must be left entirely to the judgment of the worker, who will make them longer or shorter according to the extent of surface to be covered, the abruptness of the curves, the coarseness or fineness of the material wrought upon, and the destination of the work when finished, &c. Naturally a closer stitch and more solid work are required for antimacassars or sofa-cushions, which are always coming in contact with fidgety and restless human beings, decked out with every kind of ornamental excrescence likely to pull and catch at worsted-work, than for a frieze of needlework, nailed immediately under the ceiling.*

The stitches should be smoothly and evenly laid and should resemble the woof of satin.

In working, the outline is to be covered first; for instance, in working the stalk of a flower begin from the lower end first and work on the outline till it is crossed by a leaf, or terminates in a flower; then pass the needle to the other side and work back again to the lower end; then work another line of stitches *inside* the outline till the stalk is filled up. (See Diagram 2.) Leaves that are all one colour are worked in the same way, and the veins are put in last. (See Diagram 3.)

Variegated leaves and shaded flower-petals are treated differently, though the stitch is still the same. The outer edge of colour is worked first, beginning *on* the outline and going towards the centre. Be careful not to take *all* the stitches right up to the inner edge of colour, so that the two shades may dovetail into one another, and a sharp, hard, defined line be avoided. (See Diagram 4.) It is quite easy to make curves and angles in this stitch, taking care that the lines of stitches follow the direction of the fibre or *grain* of the object imitated in needlework. Thus the stalk of a plant should never be worked *across*, as we frequently see it done, but invariably lengthwise. Old-fashioned pieces of *pictorial* embroidery may be advantageously studied in this respect, though we do not recommend our readers to imitate them in others. Good line engravings, too, will often afford useful hints as to the direction of stitches. Indeed, an embroideress will, if she loves her art, always have her eyes open, and her mind alert and ready to find instruction. It is very necessary to fill up thin places in this stitch without any appearance of patchiness. Embroidery in floss silk is executed in this way, the stitches being carefully *laid* with the piercer; this little implement is of great use in working with floss silks; it keeps the fibres open and broad, whereas

DIAGRAM 5.—SATIN STITCH.

DIAGRAM 6.—FRENCH KNOT, I.

without it they would be constantly twisting. Before the silk is pulled right through the stuff, it should be passed over and spread on the flat end of the piercer.

This kind of stitch, which the French call *point perdu*, because its beginnings and endings should, in good embroidery, be *lost* and undefined, is, of course, not available for twisted silks, which require a different treatment, and *point passé*, or satin stitch, must be adopted. This

---

* In speaking of Paolo of Verona, Vasari mentions with approbation the fact that he worked with the old-fashioned *close* stitch, which besides greater solidity had the advantage of producing an effect more like painting. "This manner of working," he goes on to say, "is now nearly forgotten, and a longer stitch has been adopted which is less durable and less agreeable to the eye."

consists in *passing* the silk from one outline to another. Those beautiful pieces of Indian and Chinese embroidery, with the right and wrong sides exactly alike (making, indeed, two *right sides*), are wrought in this manner. The piercer here again comes in usefully for keeping the stitches even and smooth. Sometimes it is desirable to *raise* certain portions of the work; this may be done with cotton, and the silk taken over the padding, as illustrated in Diagram 5. This stitch is used for embroidery over cardboard, and when the pattern is to be raised a piece of string should be sewn in the centre of the cardboard, and the silk

22.—DESIGN FOR SOFA-CUSHION, &c.

taken over it. The stitches should always be taken in a slanting direction—that is to say, they should, if possible, never run parallel to either the warp or the woof of the material.

Buttonhole stitch, coral stitch, chain stitch, knot stitch, fern stitch, &c., all of which are too well known to need description, are only used in appliqué-work, and then principally to strengthen the material that makes the pattern, and to enrich it. The French knot is used in most kinds of embroidery, and as it requires some skill, we recommend our readers to practise it first with common materials. The needle being on the right side of the stuff, you take the silk between the finger and thumb of your left hand, at a short distance from the work, with your right hand you then twist the needle round the silk, and then insert it in the stuff near to where the silk has been drawn through. The needle must then be pulled through, and the silk wound round it will form a little tube through which the whole needleful must pass and be drawn quite tight. The little tube will form the half of a sphere, and should be as smooth and round as a bead. (See Diagram 6.) In working without a frame, you do this stitch somewhat differently. A small portion of the stuff being taken, a needle is then thrust quite through the tube formed by the twisting of the silk, and when the thread it carries is also drawn through, it must be re-inserted in the stuff at the point where it was first put in. French knots are used for filling up the centres of flowers.

23.—Embroidery for the End of a Necktie.

Edging cords and gold are fastened down by fine sewing silk taken over them. When the outline is finished, a hole must be made in the stuff with a stiletto, the cord cut off and the end threaded on a large round-eyed needle, taken through the stiletto hole and fastened off securely at the back.

This is merely the stitch proper; many others are used in this work, such as feather stitch, *point russe*, satin, &c.

CHAPTER VI.

COLOUR AND DESIGN.

WE English are a colour-loving race, and our lives would be monotonous in outward seeming but for that fact. Flaming reds and gorgeous yellows, forbidden us by good taste in the details of our dresses, may be used in a subdued and decorous way in the appointments of our houses. To use these or any other colours injudiciously is to abuse them, but the greatest fault to be avoided is the use of a crude, harsh tint instead of a good, cheerful tone of any colour we employ. In our dress, too, no exhibition of crude colour should ever be allowed to appear. English ladies make a great mistake in the use of colour in their dress; we have hopes, however, that the numerous "dress reforms" and æsthetic aspirations of the present generation will result in some improvement in this particular. In Art Needlework colour is the most prominent feature, and should be studied with the utmost care and attention.

It is a difficult matter to lay down rules as to colour; we can only warn, advise, and suggest, and leave the rest to the natural taste—if she has any—of the worker. Ladies who experience any symptoms of colour-blindness should by no means attempt embroidery. Unfortunately people do not or will not know when they lack the artistic quality, and cannot understand why a scheme of colour which appears rich and harmonious enough to them should offend the eye of other people. In a choice of colour harmony must be the first consideration.

A great authority on colour says that, to be harmonious, primaries of equal intensity must exist in the proportions of 3 yellow, 5 red, and 8 blue—integrally 16. The secondaries in the proportions of 8 orange, 13 purple, 11 green—integrally 32. The tertiaries, citrine (compound of orange and green), 19; russet (orange and purple) 21; olive (green and purple) 24—integrally 64. It follows, therefore, that each secondary, being a compound of two primaries, is neutralised by the remaining primary in the same proportions—thus 8 of orange by 8 of blue, 11 of green by 5 of red, 13 of purple by three of yellow. The tertiaries are neutralised by the secondaries in the same proportion. Of course the above proportions suppose the colours to be used in their prismatic intensities; but as hundreds, we may rather say thousands, of shades and tones are in daily use in dress and decoration, we must, after all, fall back upon ourselves, our individual taste, and our experience.

This latter quality teaches us that blue and orange are harsh colours and must be used in small proportions and much tempered by more subdued tints. Greys and browns are invaluable in breaking up harsh lines and softening crude colours. Black and white used in judicious

14.—Embroidered Lamp-Mat.

quantities also possess this quality; if used injudiciously, however, they frequently act entirely by contrary, and make a decided colour even more glaring.

In the arrangement of a room one will occasionally see a brilliant antimacassar placed just where the strongest light falls upon it, rendering its otherwise good qualities almost hideous in their intensity, while if the said antimacassar had been placed in some cool, dark corner it would have been subdued, at the same time appearing a pretty spot of colour amongst its dark surroundings.

In dress, the arrangement of a home, and especially in embroidery, every seeming trifle "tells," and renders the effect good or indifferent.

An embroideress who copies from nature will often find, in making her sketch, that she will be compelled to add or diminish. A twig or branch, for instance, in nature will sometimes have on its upper side a thick cluster of leaves and flowers, while the under side is bare and

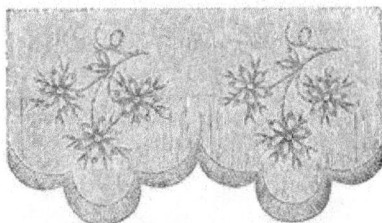

25.—EMBROIDERY FOR CHILDREN'S DRESSES.

26.—EMBROIDERED SOFA-CUSHION. FOR DETAIL SEE No. 59.

almost leafless. This will not do in embroidery; the upper side must be considerably thinned, and the under part somewhat added to, or, strange to say, though copied from nature, the effect will not seem *natural*. Another hint may be beneficial to the anxious worker. In embroidering upon a grey, cream, or any neutral-tinted ground the colours used may be much more vivid than if the surface be pure white. White materials are usually embroidered in silk.

A worker who would be an artist at her work must remember that she does not possess all an artist's privileges. In obtaining his colours he may alter or produce them by unlimited mixing, &c., but the embroideress cannot do this with her wool or silk, and must take care to use just the right tint of colour she requires, or the effect, from an artistic point of view, will

27.—EMBROIDERY FOR LAMP-MAT. No. 28.

28.—LAMP-MAT.

be a failure. In subduing and somewhat altering the shade of a colour, too, the artist has the advantage over the embroideress, who must, by the juxtaposition and proportion of her colours, gain this end for herself. Crewels and silks are now made in every shade and tint of a colour, so that if the worker has "an artist's eye" for colour she will know exactly what shade to choose so as to render her work attractive and artistic. This is another advantage over Berlin wool, in which it was not possible to obtain sufficient gradation in a colour, and for this reason the harmony of the work was frequently destroyed.

29.—BUNCH OF PELARGONIUMS.

In drawing a design no empty little spaces should be left and yet no unnatural crowding allowed to appear. To fill up a bare space a little bird, bud, or butterfly will often be found useful.

The Japanese have the art of "filling up" with very little to perfection. In studying an ordinary Japanese screen this cannot fail to impress the observant, and should be adopted as a useful hint. We English are too fond of size. We are apt to think things mean when

30.—PANSY FOR EMBROIDERY.

31.—FUCUSIA.

32.—CONVOLVULUS.

they are small, forgetting that much must necessarily be made up of little, and that the highest mountain is merely composed of a vast concourse of atoms. For this reason we choose thick clusters, large flowers and leaves, rather than—as the Japanese—merely covering the surface with as little as possible. Judgment is required in thus arranging designs for embroidery, so that in avoiding this heavy crowding our work does not fall into the opposite extreme of meagreness.

To return, however, to our primaries and secondaries. Yellow is the colour the most akin to light, and stands about midway between yellow and blue in this respect. Where you want warmth and light, there it is well to make your prevailing colour yellow.

Each primary, as is well known, has a complementary colour, composed of the other two primaries: thus, green is the complementary of red, purple of yellow, and orange of blue. A primary and its complementary form a full and harmonious contrast. The primaries, indeed,

33.—Embroidery for Writing-Mat No. 35.

reflect their complementaries in a certain proportion; as, in acoustics, when a fundamental note is sounded, its harmonies sound also. The primaries, however well proportioned in quantity and intensity, do not produce an harmonious effect, yet if the contrasts are multiplied by being repeated in small quantities, the relative proportions being observed, black and white being added, and distance and light helping to blend the component colours, a very agreeable result may be produced. The Egyptians in the decoration of their temples made use of this system of colour.

Brilliancy does not by any means depend on the primitive colours, which if not well proportioned will appear dull and heavy, as well as gaudy and discordant, while the dull and heavy tertiaries may, on the other hand, if well arranged, produce an effect almost brilliant.

Always remember that when a primary is tinged with another primary, and contrasted with a secondary, the secondary must have a tinge of the third primary. For instance : Simple red may be used with pure green; but scarlet, which is red tinged with yellow, must have a blue green; and crimson, or red tinged with blue, must have a yellow green.

Colours placed in juxtaposition react upon one another, and acquire each a tinge of the other. Neutral colours reflect the complementaries of colours on which they are placed. Neutral grey, for example, on an orange ground, acquires a tinge of blue, of which orange is the complementary colour. On a green ground the grey becomes reddish; on yellow ground, violet; on a blue ground, orange; while a neutral ground has a very subduing and harmonising effect on the colours placed on it.

34.—EMBROIDERY FOR WRITING-MAT, NO. 35.

Perspective should not be a characteristic of embroidery, the so-called "pictorial embroidery" seldom appearing short of ridiculous and unnatural. Light and shade belong to pictures. In dress and decoration textile fabrics necessarily change position and light, so that sometimes, if light and shade were used, the real light might fall upon that part you desired to remain in shadow, and the whole effect be necessarily spoiled.

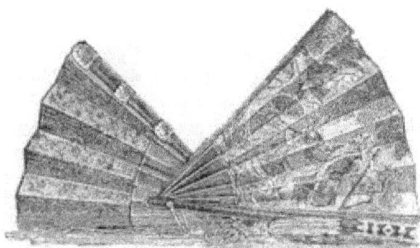

CHAPTER VII.

ARTICLES SUITABLE FOR EMBROIDERY.

THE number of objects to which embroidery may be applied are very numerous, and afford ample scope for ingenuity. Antimacassars, screens, sofa-cushions, and portières are among the most useful of the number. For bedrooms whole suites may be made, consisting of toilet mats and covers, night-dress-cases, bed-covers, watch-pockets, &c. These are most appropriately made in crash, linen, towelling and cretonne, and are an immense improvement on the ugly little crochet or dimity mats we have been doomed until lately to use. Cushions and footstools occupy, next to antimacassars, the most prominent place in embroidery, and are always to the fore among the luxuries of our rooms. Curtains, both hand and banner screens, mantelpiece valances, friezes, &c., may all be made in embroidery. Large standing-screens, in frames, if skilfully executed, look almost as well as pictures, and are admirable for decorating a room, as are also those little curtains that are occasionally placed at the open shelves of cabinets, &c.

Articles suitable for bazaars which may be made in embroidery are very numerous; among them are: penwipers, satchels, needle-cases, tea-cosies, d'oyleys, purses, and money-bags; not forgetting tobacco-pouches, cigar-cases, smoking-caps, which may be made in hundreds of designs and stuffs. It is such a difficult thing to get anything suitable to present to a gentleman, that ladies will hail these last-named as a welcome boon when birthdays or Christmas draws near. We must not forget to mention ticket-cases, scent-bags, tea-cloths, &c., &c. Aprons in every material may be embroidered upon, from coarse white linen aprons with bibs to the finest muslin, silk, or satin.

For dresses, the trimmings, when of crewel-work, should always be worked separately and put on afterwards, as the material is apt to get dragged if the pattern is worked on the foundation. If not done in this way, they have a habit of looking as if ladies had donned their tablecloths or window-curtains. Trains, ladies' waistcoats, cuirasses, petticoats, bodices, and, indeed, whole dresses, are now much trimmed with needlework. Children's dresses look especially well when embroidered in this way. It is best for even these that too many colours are not used, and that the embroidery be put on separately like trimming. These dresses may be made in crash, merino, workhouse twill, silk, satin, serge, or holland.

Aprons for carriages is another item to join the army of embroidered articles. The design should run round the edges, and these should afterwards be bound with braid or ribbon to match the colours used in the embroidery.

A brilliant design is somewhat out of place here. Variegated autumn leaves, ivy, or hops, vine leaves and tendrils are the sort of designs most suited to this purpose. The crash used will also be found of greater use if of a dark colour, as the white quickly soils and looks glaring in the sun, taking off that cool appearance so delightful when driving in the heat and dust. These carriage-rugs have the advantage of lightness as well as looking cool.

Mittens have of late taken very much the place of gloves, and may be embroidered with fine silk. Hanging pockets, scarves, sashes, fichus, and cravat-ends are all likely subjects for the needle. These may be made in silk, gauze, crêpe, tulle, or cashmere, and are almost indispensable in a lady's toilet.

Embroidered girdles and suspenders are a great improvement when used with hanging pockets.

Utrecht velvet is a very suitable material for portières or mantelpiece valances. These of course need lining, and should be finished off by a deep chenille or silk fringe, or even with thick silk lace. When a room is much ornamented with embroidery, it should harmonise in colour both with each other and the rest of the furniture. Rooms are so often spoiled by the indiscriminate use of inartistic decoration, that we hope this little hint will not be thrown away. There is also another material that is very handsome and suitable for this purpose. It is a kind of ribbed velveteen which may be had in shades of grey or brown, and when worked with crewels looks especially rich and suitable. The design for this material should be bold and decided; the material is thick, soft, and pliant to work upon. Ladies' little straw hand-bags are frequently worked in crewels, either with a spray of flowers, a bird, or the monogram or name of the owner. Sometimes the possessor, if of an eccentric turn of mind, will ornament her bag with a fish, dragon, or some quaint head, &c. Little dogs' great-coats may be worked in any fanciful design the owner chooses. We have seen a room which contained several cabinets of precious china the hangings of which were of white Utrecht velvet, and embroidered in silver, gold, and pale blue or crimson threads in a design somewhat representing the pattern of the china. The effect was singularly good. We should advise our readers to adopt it. Gold and silver are so rarely used, except for church decorations, that this makes them all the more effective and pretty when taken into account.

Slippers are acceptable to every one, except popular young curates who are burdened with an overdose of female admirers. Why curates should always be presented with slippers ever has been, and will, I fear, remain, a mystery, unless, indeed, it be that curates are usually over-worked and have little or no time to wear them. Gentlemen—or ladies either—who are at all inclined to gout or corns ever welcome these additions to their comfort, and we should strongly advise our readers to present them where they will be really acceptable, and so rid the unfortunate curate of a few of his fair tormentors. These slippers may be worked in either silk or crewels in a hundred different devices. If worked in silk, satin, or kid they are extremely handsome for ladies' dress wear. Gloves may also be embroidered in the same way. Ladies occasionally

35.—MAT FOR WRITING MATERIALS. FOR DETAILS SEE Nos. 33 and 34.

36.—EMBROIDERED READING-DESK.

37.—DESIGN FOR A SOFA-CUSHION.

38.—DETAIL OF READING-DESK No. 36.

embroider their parasols, and they look extremely well when so done, though this would be likely to form the occupation of one "whose time hung heavy on her hands," for very handsome parasols may now be obtained at most reasonable prices. A very pretty as well as essential addition to the tea-table is the cosy, which should be embroidered so as to match the table-cover both in colour and design.

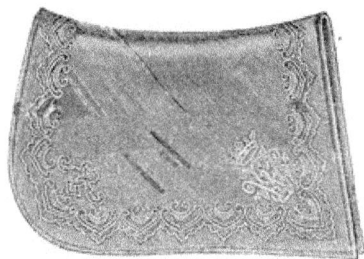

39.—SADDLE-CLOTH. FOR DETAIL SEE No. 44.

40.—WASTE-PAPER BASKET.

41.—WORK-BASKET.

42.—EMBROIDERY FOR WASTE-PAPER BASKET No. 40.

We should advise all workers to embroider upon tolerably good materials, for if not the work, time, and trouble seem as though thrown away.   The work varies according to the material used.   Of course in working upon crash or towelling the stitches would necessarily be much coarser than upon silk or even linen, and we should embroider a serge with somewhat less pains-taking than we should a satin.   Common sense will put this forth to every worker, and we need say nothing further on the subject.   In former times the bed-curtains and hangings were beautifully embroidered, and at a Kentish mansion near Penshurst a bed that was destined for King James the First cost eight thousand pounds.   The hangings were of gold and silver tissue, and lined with richly-embroidered satin.   This costly room was fitted up with chairs, stools, &c., of similar materials and design, the cost of the whole amounting to twenty thousand pounds.   Queen Elizabeth was

43.—EMBROIDERY FOR TABLE No. 49.

very proficient in the art of embroidery.   There is a room at Penshurst where the crimson chairs and couches are magnificently embroidered, and said to be the work of the Queen and her maids-of-honour.   This room was worked especially to do honour to Sir Henry Sidney.   In the Middle Ages more especially there was a rage for embroidery in England.   While the Saxons were in power the art reached its perfection; since then, we are sorry to add, there has been a general decline, and we can only hope that, as we have now begun to see the folly of our ways, we shall gradually work it up to its original glory.   Much of the embroidery of olden times was done in convents and abbeys by religious men as well as women.   This work was meant for the Church, though Royalty, struck by its beauty and worth, would occasionally demand or seize upon it to decorate the walls and ceilings of their stately palaces.   Queen Matilda is said to have extorted from the monks of Abingdon their richest vestments as a present to herself.   The famous so-called Bayeux tapestry was simply crewel-work done in long stitch on linen.   Queen Matilda

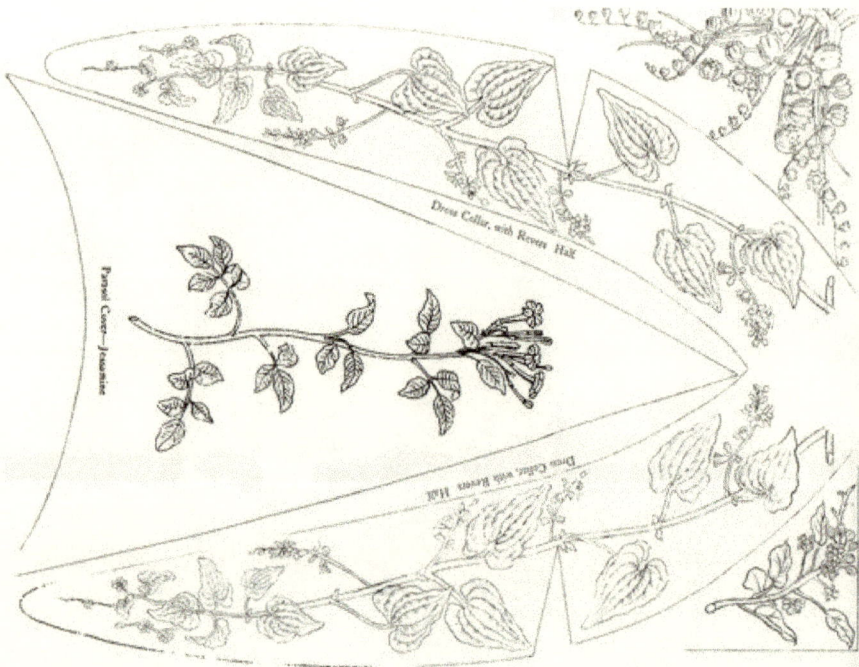

Dress Collar, with Revers Half

Parasol Cover—Jessamine

Dress Collar, with Revers Half

has the reputation of being the author of this work, but there is much room for doubt upon the subject. Both men and women pursued this art as a business, and a great trade was carried on with other countries.

At St. Mary's Church, Oxford, there is a beautiful pulpit-cloth of appliqué-work. It is of blue velvet upon a gold ground. Many beautiful examples of ancient ecclesiastical needlework are thus scattered up and down the country. In Lincoln alone there are upwards of six hundred vestments wrought in divers kinds of needlework. Not only for the church, however, was embroidery used, but also for domestic decoration. We are getting more like them ourselves in this particular.

44.—EMBROIDERY FOR SADDLE-CLOTH No. 39.

But to return to the practical. There have been several disputes as to whether the present crewel-work washes well. This is hardly a safe thing either to vouch for or deny, as so much depends upon the carefulness or otherwise of the washer. No soap or soda must be used; a little bran should be placed in warm water, and the work left to soak. Press the material every now and then, but it will not bear rubbing. When soaked long enough to render it clean do not wring it, but after shaking it so as to rid it of as much superfluous water as possible, hang it to partly dry; then either finish it by hanging it on a frame to finish, or iron it. Sometimes a little ox-gall is used as a preventive against the colours running. If the wool used be good and all these precautions strictly adhered to there is no reason whatever why the washing of crewel-work should not be entirely satisfactory.

Perambulator-aprons are articles that may be embroidered; also counterpanes, and even the

D

backs of pianos. There is a twilled sheeting very suitable for counterpanes; it is 72 inches wide, and costs 2s. 6d. per yard. This material is thick and handsome, and quite pays for any trouble expended upon it.

If worked in a design to imitate peacocks' feathers, with a bunch of large ones to form a centre, and smaller worked round for a border, it would be very pretty and effective. Flowers, scrolls, or, indeed, any design, is quite as suitable if preferred. Imagine a scarf of white satin for an evening dress worked in tobacco-flowers and maidenhair fern. The pattern should be represented by a handsome bunch in front, a few sprays of fern, and then a smaller bunch, and so on all

45.—Embroidered Medallion.

round, the smaller bunches and sprays of fern forming festoons, not running straight round, for if so the drapery of the scarf would render it impossible to show the full design. This design would be even more effective if worked on black satin. Violets are always a pretty design for embroidery. An apron, bodice, train, pocket, &c., look charming when worked in little bunches of white and blue violets. Roses always form a large portion of every representation of flowers, and they are much used in crewel-work. A lawn tennis dress of écru flannel, with trimming of moss-rose buds and leaves, is acknowledged by most people to be as near perfection as possible. Forget-me-nots also come in for their share of approbation, together with myrtle, apple-blossoms, &c., and many kinds of fruits. Any one in possession of an old-fashioned marble-topped chiffonier might modernise it by having panels at the sides of serge or satin, worked in silk or crewels, and covering the top with the same. The edge should have a deep fringe. Quite a modern elegant article is thus obtained by a little trouble and ingenuity. The hop-plant is a very good design for the embroiderer's needle, and is suitable for nearly everything. It may be mixed with almost any flower, and the tendrils have always a graceful and artistic effect. Ottomans can be covered with crewel-work, and are far less trouble and much more effective than Berlin wool-work. Appliqué-work is one of the most charming and effective of trimmings for

46.—EMBROIDERED MEDALLION.

dresses, dolmans, &c. We have seen a dress of dark blue cashmere which was richly embroidered with grey appliqué-work. The embroidery was of thick velvet, and seemed to be raised from the cashmere. The effect was very rich and pretty. On dolmans, mantles, &c., if the work is applied in black velvet upon silk or satin, it always looks handsome and *distingué*. Mantelpiece valances look especially well when done in appliqué-work, as well as heavier things, such as curtains, portières, &c.

Little things are also embroidered in this way, slippers, cosies, cushions, &c., and, when skilfully cut and carefully embroidered, generally prove satisfactory. If we sit down to our work merely with the idea of gaining amusement, and no higher motive or ambition, we had better let Art Needlework alone, and content ourselves with crochet and Berlin wool-work. If, on the contrary, we think it worthy of a better attention and greater study, we shall find that it just fills a void that we never could before satisfy, and we shall look upon our work with the same eye as the painter looks at his picture, and handle it with as delicate a touch as the musician fingers his keys.

An old proverb says, "Nothing is worth doing at all that is not worth doing well." And this applies to Art Needlework especially. To lose one's temper over one's work and tear or drag the material is to utterly spoil the smooth picture-like effect which is our highest ambition to gain; patience and perseverance are needed here as in most things, and without it little will be effected. We might sum up the rules for needlework under these heads :—Patience, harmony, cleanliness, and careful handling. There are so many things that are spoiled from the want of cleanliness and delicate handling that we hope that this hint will not be thrown away. To have skill is to be rich in a good thing, but this every one has not, especially at the beginning of their undertaking; it is more a thing that grows upon us, gradually lifting us out of that mere mechanical sphere of action that we seem at first called upon to inhabit.

Improvement at least invariably follows steady application, and we should give as our advice to all workers to start with patience, keep pace with perseverance, outrun labour, conquer difficulty, and never stop till skill and ingenuity are fairly yours. Time only can effect this; no one can reach perfection at a stroke; indeed, if we could it would hardly seem worth the reaching, it being the very striving after its attainment which constitutes its value. No woman—if she has time, of course—should be above fancy work; indeed, we fancy such a one to be lacking in feminine qualities, and certainly in artistic taste. A woman who is proficient in fancy work saves a small fortune, and has always the means of beautifying her home literally at her fingers'-ends. The cultivation of the beautiful in any form cannot fail to be praiseworthy and ennobling.

CHAPTER VIII.

NOS. 1 and 3. Work-Basket. (Embroidery.) Work-basket of thin split cane, covered with turkey red plush, embroidered and trimmed with gold braid. For the embroidery trace on the plush the pattern given in Illustration 3, and work the embroidery in chain stitch, interlacing buttonhole stitch, and point russe. The flowers are worked alternately with several shades of blue and of reseda, and the buds with pink silk. The veining is worked with gold thread, and the raised spots and stamens with pieces cut out of the braid. The tendrils and sprays are worked with olive silk. The centre of the lid, where the cane is open-worked, is threaded with the gold braid. The handle is wound round with twisted silk and tassels, and a narrow fringe is sewn round the lid. Rosettes and tassels of silk, as shown in Illustration 1.

No. 2. Hop-leaf and tendrils suitable for Embroidery in Crewel Wool. The leaf is in pale-green crewel wool, with thick veinings of the same shade. The tendrils are, if anything, a trifle paler, and the stalk is in the same shade.

Nos. 4 and 5. Waste-Paper Basket. Cardboard basket with thin canes covered with canvas, and wound round with black leather. At the back is a bronze ring by which the basket is hung up. The front of the basket has a circular piece of embroidery on a ground of pale grey cloth. Trace the pattern and embroider the swan and water in silks and crewels, the former in silver-grey, the latter in a bluish tint. The edge and leaves are green. The sewing on of the embroidery is hidden by a bronze ring.

Nos. 6, 10, and 12. Ornamental Work-Basket. The basket is made of wood and cardboard covered with a light straw, lined with red satin, and fitted up with pockets to match. The sewing on of the lining and straps is hidden by ruchings and rosettes of red satin ribbon. The foundation, sides, and cross-piece of the basket are of wood, and the ends of cardboard, with satin sides, as shown in Illustration 6, which represents the basket open. In No. 12 the design for the embroidery is given in the original size. When the pattern has been drawn the roses are embroidered with crewels or split filoselle in four shades of pink, and the blossoms with

47.—Writing-Case.

48.—Garden Basket.

49.—Embroidered Table. For Detail see No. 43.

50.—Butter Basket.

51.—Detail of No. 50.

white. The wheatears are worked in chain stitch with maize-coloured filoselle or crewel wool and gold thread. The stems consist of gold cord sewn on with silk of the same shade. The

51.—DETAIL OF No. 54.

53.—DETAIL OF No. 54.

54.—EMBROIDERED CARD-RACK. FOR DETAILS SEE NOS. 51 & 53.

55.—DETAIL OF DUSTER-BASKET, No. 50.

leaves and sprays are worked with many shades of green and brown filoselle, or crewels in overcast and feather stitch, and plain and interlacing satin stitch. The lining is slightly wadded and quilted. The handle of straw and cardboard is covered with a leaf-like pleating of red satin.

Nos. 7 and 8. Penwiper. (Embroidery.) The foundation of this penwiper is made of cardboard 4 inches long by 2⅞ wide, and bound round the edge with black silk braid. On

56.—EMBROIDERY FOR CHAIR-BACKS, &c.

to the cord is sewn a square of stiffened muslin 4 inches in diameter, rounded towards the centre, so that it only measures 2½ there. (See Illustration 8.) It is covered outside with blue satin, on which is sewn a piece of fine white flannel, embroidered with coloured crewels or silk, in the pattern given in No. 7. Trace the design upon the flannel, and work the flowers for chain stitch with red, blue, and pink silks, the tendrils and foliage with olive silk in satin and overcast stitch. Then turn down the blue satin, and sew round the edge a double line of gold thread with overcast stitches of blue silk. A white silk fringe is sewn on under the embroidery. A thick cord of blue silk is sewn round the foundation and continued to form the handles. The ends are then filled up with loose-pleated ruchings of black cloth cut

57.—Design for Table-Cover Borders.

round the edge with small vandykes. Similar cloth is then sewn on underneath the cardboard foundation.

Nos. 9 and 11. Embroidered Sachet. Materials required: Cardboard, cotton wool, grey taffetas, and coloured silks or crewels. The cardboard is cut into two squares, each measuring 12 inches. On the wrong side they are wadded and scented, and then covered on both sides with silver-grey taffetas. The outer side is embroidered, the illustration of which we give in

No. 11.   After the pattern has been traced upon the taffetas the rosebuds are worked with

58.—EMBROIDERY FOR CARD-TRAY.

three shades of silks or crewels, and the ivy-leaves in green.   The stems and sprays are embroidered with green and brown silks in crewel stitch and *point russe.* The border is worked

59.—EMBROIDERY FOR SOFA-CUSHION No. 16.

in grey of different shades in knotted stitch and *point russe,* and is relieved with fine gold cord sewn on with black stitches. A strip of grey taffetas 2½ inches broad is then gathered at each side and used to join the two halves of the sachet, one side being left open so as to admit of handkerchiefs, laces, &c., being placed within them. The sachet is then finished off with grey silk cord and a ruching of grey sarcenet ribbon. Button and loop to fasten.

Nos. 13 and 14. Ornamental Basket with Embroidery. Circular frame of bronze standing

60.—BOX FOR WRITING MATERIALS. FOR DETAIL SEE NO. 61.

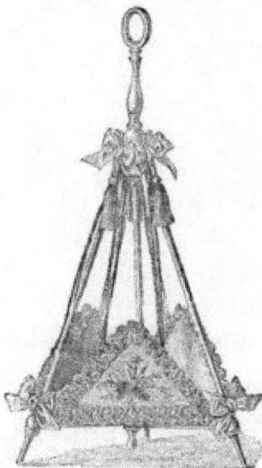

61.—CARD-BASKET.

10 inches high, including the handle. It has a strip of cardboard covered with lilac satin and white cloth placed round the frame. No. 14 gives the design in its original size. When the pattern has been traced upon the satin the blossoms are embroidered with white, yellow, and cerise in chain stitch and *point russe*. The buds are pink and green, and worked in satin stitch; the stems and sprays are brown, and worked in feather stitch and *point russe*. Along

the scallops is sewn a light blue silk braid and gold cord; the cloth is then cut away and the basket finished off with ruchings of blue satin ribbon. A blue silk cord and tassels trim the handle.

Nos. 15 and 17. Work-Basket. The material selected is black polished cane; the basket

61.—EMBROIDERED FOOTSTOOL. FOR DETAIL SEE No. 69.

63.—HAND SCREEN. FOR DETAIL SEE No 64

rests on four feet and is fitted with handles of red silk, and is finished off by tassels. It is lined with pieces of cardboard covered on the outside with écru-coloured silk, which shows through the open-work of the canes. On the inside these pieces are covered with scarlet silk which has been previously wadded and quilted into small diamonds. In Illustration 17 we give the design for the grey cloth with silk or crewels for crewel stitch. The poppies are worked in red, the cornflowers blue, and the asters in white. The stamina are worked with yellow in knotted stitch, and the wheatears in finely split straw in crewel stitch. The buds, leaves, and branches are worked with green and brown in crewel stitch and *point russe*. The sewing on of the embroidered portion is hidden by red silk gimp.

No. 16. Toilet-Cushion. Square cushion, five inches wide, covered with blue satin; in the centre is a square of linen gauze embroidered as follows:—The flowers with white and

64.—EMBROIDERY FOR BOX, No. 60.

blue silk, in chain and knotted stitch and point russe; the leaves with two shades of olive silk, in crewel and overcast stitch. For the open-worked pattern draw out every 10 threads one way, and cross every 4 of the threads left standing with grey silk. Round the edges of this pattern work a row of buttonhole stitch with blue silk; the cross stitches on the outside are worked with the same silk. Then line the embroidery with blue satin, so that the satin forms a narrow band round the linen gauze, and add the bows of blue satin ribbon, folded as shown in our illustration.

Nos. 18 and 20. Low Chair of Fancy Straw, upholstered with silk plush embroidered in crewel stitch. The chair itself is gilt of a dull tint of gold, and the cushion for the seat should measure 4 inches high. It is loose from the chair, but the cushions for the back and sides are upholstered in the regular way with buttons. A coloured braid, with tassels, is sewn round the plush, and a cord of the corresponding colour round the cushion. No. 18 gives the design for the embroidery, which is worked on the plush in crewel stitch with coloured silks. The small covers for the arms are embroidered to correspond.

Nos. 19 and 21. Ornamental Stand for Books, Music, Pictures, &c. The framework of

65.—DETAIL OF BAG No. &c.

polished cane has an oval embroidery, the original size of which is given in No. 21. The design is worked on a design of white satin with purse silks and fine chenille of various colours, part of the embroidery being executed in crewel, feather, and knotted stitch. The rose has four shades of red chenille, the asters white chenille and white silk. The violets and forget-me-nots are worked with violet and blue chenille, with stamens of yellow silk. The leaves, sprays, and tendrils are embroidered in brown and green, partly with chenille, partly with silk.

No. 22. Design for Embroidery in Crewel Stitch. This is intended for the centre of a

66.—DETAIL OF No. 47.

67.—EMBROIDERY FOR SMOKING-CAP.

sofa or carriage cushion, or it may be employed for a wall-pocket or blotting-book, or even a waste-paper basket. Either silks or crewels may be used. The poppies a deep bright red, forget-me-nots pale blue with yellow centres, the leaves of one or two well-chosen shades

66.—DETAIL OF SCREEN No. 63.

69.—EMBROIDERY FOR FOOT-REST No. 61.

of green. The two circles in the centre of the design should be in old gold. If worked entirely in white cotton this design is very effective as an ornament for a nightdress or pillow-case.

No. 23.   Design for the End of a Cravat. The design, of which we give the original size,

70.—LOUIS SEIZE FOOTSTOOL.

71.—DETAIL OF CUSHION No. 71.

is embroidered with coloured purse silks on crossway pieces of white grosgrain silk, the stitches used crewel, overcast, knotted, and feather stitch.

No. 24.   Embroidered Screen or Lamp-Mat. This screen is embroidered on black cashmere. It may also be used for a cushion or sachet. The pattern consists of a bunch of cornflowers and ears of corn. The latter are embroidered in satin stitch in two shades of yellow silk, or in crewel stitch with crewel wool. The long stitches are worked with gold thread, as also are the stems. The flowers consist of one white stitch and two blue stitches. The veinings are worked with gold thread. The cup has an outline of gold thread, with a green and wood-coloured framework. The poppies are worked in satin stitch, with red silk for the petals, the centre in buttonhole

72.—EMBROIDERED CUSHION. FOR DETAIL SEE No. 73.

73.—DETAIL OF CUSHION No. 74.

stitch, with yellow silk and point d'armes in wood-colour. The foliage is worked in different shades of green, the stems with gold thread. The small flowers are yellow, red, and white. The octagon border imitates a brocaded braid. The pattern consists of yellow stars and red diamonds, with gold centres. The long stitches between the diamonds are worked with white silk. The screen is mounted on bamboo, and ornamented with tassels of different colours.

No. 25. Border for Children's Dresses. Ground, White Piqué. The pattern is worked with turquoise blue ice wool in chain, overcast, and feather stitch. The outer edge is worked in buttonhole stitch.

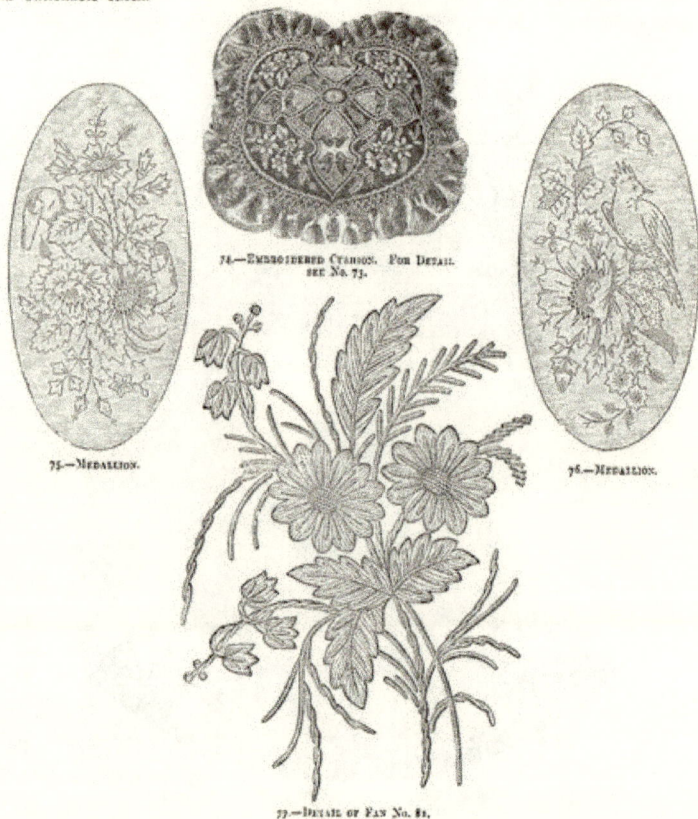

74.—EMBROIDERED CUSHION. FOR DETAIL.
SEE No. 73.

75.—MEDALLION.

76.—MEDALLION.

77.—DETAIL OF FAN No. 81.

Nos. 26 and 59. Sofa-Cushion. (Crewel Stitch and Point Russe.) Square cushion covered with bronze satin merveilleux, with embroidery worked on a ground of bronze velvet. In the centre the cushion is quilted down with small buttons of brown satin, and round the edge the satin is arranged in reversed pleatings. The design for the embroidery is transferred on to the velvet from No. 59, which represents a section in the original size. The asters are worked with two shades of rose silk in crewel stitch; the stamina in knotted stitch with gold silk. The outer leaves of the cup-shaped flower are worked with three shades of olive silk in chain stitch;

78.—MAT. FOR DETAIL SEE No. 81.

79.—WORKSTAND.

80.—WORK-BAG. FOR DETAIL SEE No. 65.

81.—DETAIL OF MAT No. 78.

the other petals in different shades of heliotrope, outlined with the same colour in overcast stitch. In the centre of this flower lines of yellow silk are worked diagonally, and crossed where they meet with brown silk. The sprays of leaves are worked with two shades of blue silk in overcast stitch; the tendrils are worked in overcast stitch with olive silk, and the blossoms in knotted stitch with yellow silk. The buttonhole stitches round the scalloped edges are worked with old-gold silk. When the design is finished the velvet is cut away from the work, so as to leave the square represented in No. 26, and after it has been slightly wadded it is sewn to the cushion. Round the outer edge is a frill of satin 2 inches wide, and at each corner a bow and ends of the same material.

Nos. 27 and 28. Embroidered Lamp-Mat. Circular mat of blue satin, with a border of fine white flannel and ruching of blue satin ribbon. The centre is cut out of satin, stiffened net, and blue cashmere for lining, and measures 10 inches in diameter. The centre is quilted in small diamonds with blue silk. The border, of which No. 27 gives a section, is embroidered

81.—EMBROIDERED FAN. FOR DETAIL SEE No. 77.

in white flannel, and vandyked round the outer edge. The cornflowers, forget-me-nots, and sprays are worked with blue, white, and green silks respectively in chain and crewel stitch. The border is then sewn on, and the mat strengthened with a ribbon wire. Round the centre is a pleated ruching of blue satin ribbon.

No. 29 shows a bunch of pelargoniums, which, when worked in crewels or silks, would form a handsome centre for a sofa-cushion, music-stool, antimacassar, &c. The petals of paler tints should be worked in faint pink shades, while the darker ones are in deep red, or else the light petals white, with deep purple shadings. The leaves are worked in shades of green, and the little buds at the left side are worked in pink and white, just tipped with dark red or purple shadings.

No. 30. Pansy for Embroidering a little Hand-Bag, &c. The paler petals worked in marone, the darker shadings deep purple, and the centre yellow. The leaves and stalk are green, with deeper-coloured veinings.

Nos. 31 and 32. Fuchsia and Convolvulus for working the corners of an Antimacassar,

Sofa-cushion, &c. The paler petals of the fuchsia are worked in a shade of pinkish white (pink silk, almost covered with white, would be suitable if the desired colour could not be obtained), the darker parts are in purple. The stamens should be worked in pale pink with red anthers. The leaves are pale green, with dark veinings. The convolvulus is pale blue, with white shadings inside the cup. The stamens are yellow. The little bud is almost purple, with mauve for the light shadings, and the leaves and tendrils are in green silk.

Nos. 33, 34, and 35. Mat for Writing Materials. Oblong mat of olive-green cloth, scalloped round the edge, and lined with the same material. A border, the design of which may be taken either from No. 33 or 34, is worked round the edge. If the pattern is taken from No. 35, a narrow black braid, woven with coloured silks, is arranged down the centre of

83.—EMBROIDERED SCREEN.

the pattern. The double lines are worked with fawn-coloured silk in interwoven buttonhole stitch, and the intervals are filled up with vandykes of fawn-coloured silks. The chain stitches are worked with two shades of fawn-coloured silks. The pattern in No. 34 is worked on a ground perforated with small holes; the chain stitches are worked with several shades of olive. The silk braid in the centre is worked across with three shades of pink and blue silk, so as to form a diamond pattern.

Nos. 36 and 38. Reading-Desk. Reading-desk of dark polished wood and gilt cane. In the centre is an oval filled up with dark green velvet on which is embroidered the design given in the original size in No. 38. When the pattern has been traced upon the ground the design is worked in crewels or silks. The flowers are in white and the buds pink. The inner part of the flowers is worked in olive silk in knotted stitch. The calices are worked in satin stitch in pale olive, crossed with a darker shade. The foliage is embroidered in several shades of maize and olive in satin and crewel stitch and *point russe*,

When the embroidery is completed the oval is lined with cardboard and a bright green lutestring.

No. 37. Designs in Crewels for Sofa-Cushions, Settees, Arm-Chairs, &c. This pattern is worked partly in satin stitch and partly in the so-called long or crewel stitch placed in rows one within another. The materials used are crewels and filoselle silk of different shades.

Nos. 39 and 44. Saddle-Cloth. (Embroidery.) Saddle-cloth of navy blue cloth lined with black felt, and embroidered with three shades of grey-blue silk in chain and interlacing button-hole stitch. The long chain stitches are crossed with gold thread. In the front corners is a small pattern worked with the same colours and in the same design as the border. In the corners at the back a monogram and crown are worked. No. 44 shows the former in the original size. The letters are worked with blue-grey silk in satin stitch, and are edged with

84.—TOWEL IN OUTLINE STITCH.

gold cord. The W is worked with feather-stitching of coloured silk, and the G knotted stitch of gold thread. The monogram is intermingled with a spray of oak-leaves and acorns; the leaves in three shades of olive, the stems and tendrils with brown silks in crewel stitch. The acorns are worked in crewel stitch with olive silk, and the cups with two shades of brown, in crewel and knotted stitch. The crown is embroidered with blue-grey silk in crewel stitch edged with gold cord, and sewn on in overcast stitch with silk of the same colour.

Nos. 40 and 42. Waste-Paper Basket. Basket of osier and polished cane, studded with bronze plates. The basket is lined and covered with very dark red cloth, which is embroidered on the outside in the design given in No. 42. The smaller flowers are worked with blue and olive crewels in buttonhole stitch; the larger with two shades of pink; the leaves and tendrils with buttonhole, overcast, and feather stitch of two shades of olive. The cloth is then lined with a thin sheet of wadding, and sewn on to the lid. The sides are embroidered with a similar pattern in the same colours. Round each section of the embroidery is a twisted cord of dark red and ivory wool.

No. 41. Work-Basket. Basket of fancy straw and black polished cane. The open-work part of the basket is threaded with blue satin ribbon, on which are sewn droppers of blue silk. The oval surface of the lid is covered with blue satin, and is fitted with small packets of needles. Above these packets of needles is a cushion covered with folds of blue satin, and trimmed round with pleatings of the same material. It has also embroidery worked on a ground of white cloth. The embroidery is worked in chain and feather stitch with pink and olive silks, and in knotted stitch with gold thread. The lower lid has a similar kind of border. Blue silk cord and tassels and bows and ends of blue satin ribbon are then added.

85.—EMBROIDERED TABLE-COVER.

Nos. 43 and 49. Occasional Table. (Embroidered cover.) Low trefoil-shaped table covered with dull crimson satin embroidered from the design given in No. 43 in satin and overcast stitch. The blossoms of edelweiss are embroidered with white chenille in satin stitch, the centre being worked with yellow silk, crossed in overcast stitches of brown filoselle. The calices are worked with grey-green silk in satin stitch, and the grasses in *point russe* with brown filoselle. The leaves, stems, and tendrils are worked with various shades of olive-green in satin and overcast stitch. The embroidery is then edged with a heavy cord and fringe of the same colour as the satin.

Nos. 45 and 46. Medallions for Note-Books, Card-Cases, Purses, &c. The designs may be worked on various materials, such as silk, leather, velvet, &c., in outline stitch. The stitch may also be worked upon cambric or muslin in black silk.

Nos. 47 and 66. Box for Writing Materials. This box, which is intended for holding writing utensils, together with paper, envelopes, and a blotter, is covered with bronze plush on the outside, and inside with the same coloured satin. It is fitted with a lock and bronze mountings. The satin which covers the top of the writing mat is embroidered with a wreath and monogram with silks in crewel and stem stitch with gold cantille. The lining for the lid has a satin ribbon sewn on in loops, into which the writing utensils are thrust.

No. 48. Garden Basket. Basket of Roman straw, fitted with a bag netted with écru-coloured thread and drawn up with écru-coloured cord and tassels. On the basket a bouquet

D.—DETAIL OF MAT No. 1)

of flowers is worked in crewel wool in satin, overcast, chain stitch, and *point russe*. The colours used are pink, blue, and yellow for the flowers, and for the leaves several shades of olive.

Nos. 50, 51, and 55. Duster Basket. Basket of willow straw and black polished cane, ornamented with three plush vandykes, joined together and finished with woollen balls, tufts, and tassels. The plush is embroidered from the design given in Nos. 51 and 55. The middle vandyke is embroidered from No. 55. Trace the design on peacock-blue plush and work it with split silk in crewel stitch. The buds and flowers are pale pink and pale blue, the calices, leaves, and branches with olive-green. The stamina are worked with olive silk in knotted stitch. The design is outlined with gold cord sewn on with fine yellow silk. The side vandykes are of bronze-brown plush embroidered from No. 51 in pink, blue, heliotrope, and olive-green, in the same style as No. 55. A woollen border of tufts of peacock-blue and bronze edges the vandykes with tassels of the same. The embroidered plush is next sewn to the basket, which is ornamented with woollen balls and tassels.

Nos. 52, 53, and 54. Embroidered Card-Rack. Cut out three oval pieces of cardboard, cover them on both sides with red satin (the centre cover must be embroidered). Sew a red

87.—DETAIL OF MAT No. 90.

cord round the edge and stitch them together; then cut a large piece of cardboard for the back corresponding in shape with the front; cover this also with red satin, and sew a cord at the edge. Make the sidepieces of double satin; pleat them at the bottom and sew them to back and front. Ornament the bottom with a red bow to hide the joinings of the front pieces. Nos. 52 and 53 show the designs on the lower ovals.

No. 56. The figures are worked in interlacing satin stitch, either separately or together, on a ground of longcloth. The wrong side is then brushed over with a solution of clear gum, and when this is dry the pattern is cut out close to the edge, and sewn like an appliqué design on to a ground of olive serge. The outlines are then gone over with gold cord, which is continued to form the tendrils.

No. 57. Design for Border of Table-Covers, &c. Ground of old-gold satin. Trace the pattern on the satin and go over the outlines with brown filoselle sewn on with brown silk. Fill up the space between the double lines with feather stitching of fine olive silk in two shades, and work round the outer edge with slanting buttonhole stitches of old-gold silk worked far

58.—EMBROIDERED WINDOW-DRAPERY.

apart. The leaf patterns are worked alternately with two shades of lilac, blue, yellow, and pink silk in slanting buttonhole stitch. The brown lines of chain stitch at each side are filled up in maize silk in herring-bone stitch, and the space between is filled with alternate leaves of olive and pale yellow silk, and with designs worked in overcast, knotted, and crewel stitch with olive, brown, and red silk.

Nos. 60 and 64. Case for Writing-Paper. (Embroidery.) The case is covered plain with dark red plush, with embroidery worked upon the lid from the pattern given in

No. 64. Narrow straps of red leather are gummed down each side of the case. Two handles of bronze and a lock of the same metal are found respectively on the sides and front. The case is divided inside into several compartments, to receive note-paper of different sizes, envelopes, post-cards, &c. The embroidery pattern is traced upon écru-coloured linen which has been previously gummed on to paper. The pattern is then cut with careful comparison of the illustration and gummed upon the red plush ground. For the embroidery

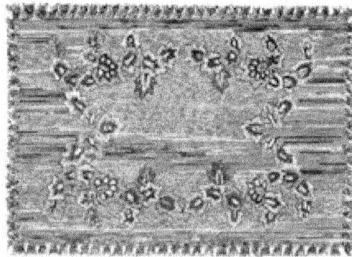

89.—MAT. FOR DETAIL SEE No. 86.

90.—MAT. FOR DETAIL SEE No. 87.

proceed as follows :—The centre bud at the top and the flower on each side of it are worked in satin stitch with several shades of pink silk, the small 5-petalled flower with heliotrope, the raised spots and lower tendrils with olive silk. The bell-shaped flowers are worked with blue, the calyx being put in with brown silk. The linen ground at the sides of these flowers is crossed with blue silk threads and the centre with gold, the threads in each case being sewn down with silk of the same colour. The veins and stamina, stems and tendrils are all worked with gold thread. Lastly, every outline is edged with gold cord, sewn on with silk of the same colour.

Nos. 58 and 61. Embroidered Card-Tray. The tray is fitted into a light frame of gilt reeds by means of blue silk cord and tassels. The three triangles are cut out of cardboard, covered with white cloth and lined with white taffetas. The cornflowers and forget-me-nots are embroidered with blue, and the wheatears with yellow silk in crewel stitch. The heath is worked in knotted stitch with red purse silk. The sprays and tendrils are embroidered with green and brown silks in crewel, overcast, and feather stitch. A ruching of pale blue sarcenet ribbon runs round each triangle, and hides the sewing on of the lining. Bows of blue grosgrain silk are then tied at the corners and among the tassels, as shown in Illustration 61.

91.—TAPESTRY MAT. FOR DETAIL SEE No. 111.

Nos. 62 and 69. Footstool. (Embroidery.) Oblong footstool of dark brown polished wood upholstered in peacock-blue plush. Down the centre is a pattern embroidered on a fawn-coloured material resembling figured damask; and this embroidery hangs down at each end of the footstool like a tab. A section of the pattern is given in No. 69, and it is worked as follows :—The pattern on the ground is filled up in crewel stitch with coloured wools, and outlined partly with a contrasting colour of silk in chain stitch, and partly with long single stitches of wool or silk. The vandykes on each side of the border are worked with peacock and olive wool, outlined with red-brown and yellow silk. The tabs are rounded and edged with a knotted fringe of peacock-blue wool, finished off with tassels of red and peacock-blue silk. The footstool is then edged with a row of silk balls (pompons) of the same colours. Larger balls and tassels are sewn on at each corner.

Nos. 63 and 68. Embroidery for a Screen. This screen is embroidered upon grass linen. The bunch in the middle is in silk. The rosebuds are in three shades of pink, the forget-me-not in three shades of blue, the leaves in olive-green, the stalks brown. The surrounding pattern is worked in yellow silk cord, *piquée* with cerise. The rest is in point russe blue stars crossed with yellow and olive palm-leaves. The canvas is lined with taffetas and mounted silk, cord, and tassels.

Nos. 65 and 80. Work-Bag. (Appliqué and Crewel Work.) The bag is cut out of a piece of olive-green satin, and measures 11 inches by 23. It is folded in half and the front part is embroidered from the pattern given in the original size in No. 65. Trace the pattern upon the satin and cut it out of olive-green velvet, which is edged by gold cord sewn on with silk of the same colour. Similar cord is sewn on in straight lines and vandykes below the appliqué. The spray of flowers is worked in crewel stitch, overcast, knotted stitch, and point russe. The rosebuds are embroidered with pink silk, and the calices, leaves, and stems with

91.—EMBROIDERED SOFA-CUSHION.

several shades of brown and olive. The blossoms are worked with fine red chenille. The satin is then lined with silk or sateen of the same colour, and the sides of the bag sewn together. It is drawn up at the top with a fine cord and tassels of olive-green silk.

No. 67. Embroidery for Smoking-Cap. Smoking-cap of dark blue velvet, slightly wadded and lined with black lutestring. The velvet is embroidered from the pattern we give in No. 67 in the original size. It is worked with four shades of bronze silk in crewel, knotted, overcast, and feather stitch, the arabesques being worked in the darker and blossoms in the lighter shade. The flowers edged with overcast stitch are filled up with crossway lines of white silk sewn with the same colour where the lines meet; the remaining part of the flower is worked in satin and chain stitch. The crown of the cap is embroidered to correspond with the border.

No. 70. Footstool Embroidered and Made in Louis the Sixteenth style. This stool may either figure as a footstool or as a music-stool. The foundation is of red plush, and the wreath of roses is in all shades—pink, red, damask white, tea, and *gloire de Dijon*. The foliage is in different shades of green, and the ribbon, which edges and winds in and out among the flowers, is in three shades of blue. To truthfully represent this style all the colours of the crewels or silk should be a little faded. The wood of the footstool is black, with gilt tracings, or, if the owner choose, it may be entirely gilt.

93.—Embroidered Towel.

94.—Embroidery for Towel No. 93.

Nos. 71 and 72. Sofa-Cushion. (Embroidery.) Oblong cushion covered with peacock-blue velvet, edged with silk cord, and finished off with pompons of coloured wool and silk at the corners. The cover on the outer side is turned back *en revers*, faced with bronze velvet, and embroidered in plain and interlacing satin stitch with faint colours of filoselle.

The cushion left free by this revers of the cover is hidden under a triangular piece of peacock-blue velvet, embroidered with filoselle in the same stitches as the revers. The outlines of the leaf patterns in the corner are worked with brown and dark reseda filoselle and filled in with

55.— EMBROIDERED CUSHION.

96.—CREWEL DESIGN.

several shades of reseda silk in *point de riz*, as shown in No. 71. The same illustration also shows the method of embroidering a flower and bud. The cushion is then finished off with a silk cord of the colours used in the embroidery.

F

Nos. 73 and 74. Circular Cushion covered round the edge with puffings of yellow silk. In the centre is a circular piece of olive-green velvet, slightly scalloped and embroidered from the design given in No. 73. The flowers are worked with pink, white, and blue silks, and the leaves with various shades of olive-green in satin, overcast, and knotted stitch. The 4 lines

97.—EMBROIDERY FOR BASKET WORK-STAND No. 106.

are made with braid of silk and gold thread, and the knotted stitches between them are worked with pale bronze silk. The double lines in the centre are also formed with the braid, and the plaited stitch and point russe worked with blue silk. For the patterns between the flowers the velvet is cut away and the space filled up with old-gold satin edged with two rows of pearl cord. The patterns on the satin are outlined with overcast stitches and filled up in plaited stitch or crossed lines. The upper figure is worked with heliotrope, the lower with brown, and the centre with olive silk. Round the embroidery is a braid and netted fringe of brown silk. The braid is worked in cross stitch with yellow silk.

Nos. 75 and 76. Medallions for Note-Books, Card-Cases, Purses, &c.

Nos. 77 and 82. Embroidered Fan. Fig. 1. The frame is of black fretwood covered with black satin embroidered with silver thread and black floss silk in chain stitch. The fan has silver mountings. Fig. 2. Frame of carved white ivory covered with white silk, and worked in white floss silk and gold cantille. It is worked in crewel and stem stitch from No. 77. A

93.—EMBROIDERED PRAYER-BOOK COVER.

border of marabout feathers, twisted white silk, and gold cantille cord with tassels, finishes the fan. Fig. 3. Frame of carved gilt wood covered with black satin, embroidered in crewel and stem stitch with different-coloured floss silks. Border of gold lace, and tassels of black silk twisted with gold. Fig. 4. Frame of polished black wood with gold designs, covered with almond satin, and a border of hen-feathers and gold beads.

Nos. 78 and 81. Mat (South Kensington Pattern). Square mat of fine holland, fringed out all round, and having a border in punto tirato. For the latter, draw out a sufficient number of threads and work one side like an open hem, taking in six threads at a time. On the other side 3 threads of the first 6 must be taken with 3 threads of the second 6, and so on. For the embroidery in the centre see No. 81, which represents it in the original size. The flowers are worked with pink crewels in buttonhole and interlacing satin stitch, the stems, calices, and stamina in satin, and overcast with marone crewels. The leaves are worked in satin and overcast stitch, with two shades of green and two of red-brown crewels. The pattern is especially suited for dinner-mats.

No. 79. Work-Basket of Willow Work, mounted upon a bamboo cane stand, and edged at the top with straw braid. The embroidery on the front consists of appliqué of cretonne covered with satin stitch in blue, pink, white, and red silk. The bag itself is old-gold satin, drawn up with

99.—CASE FOR LETTER-PAPER.

100.—EMBROIDERED TABLE-COVER.

a cord to match. Round the bamboo stand is twisted a gold cord, and the fringes and tassels should match in colours the embroidery.

No. 83. Embroidered Screen. Three-leaved screen, covered with olive velvet, embroidered with crewels and silk. The irises are worked in shaded yellow-brown silk, the leaves and stalks in olive and brownish wools. The embroidery should be lined and then nailed on the screen, with a woollen fringe border all round. The nails should have handsome gilt heads. A woollen fringe edges the bottom of the screen.

No. 84. Antimacassar. (Outline Stitch and Point Russe.) Ground of white oatmeal cloth embroidered with purse silk and crewels. For the sedge and grass, and the branch below the little landscape, several shades of olive silk and crewel are used. The water is worked with blue-grey and the swan with white silk, the boy's blouse is worked with blue and his hat with yellow silk, the girl's dress with brown and lilac silks, the apron with yellow, and the bonnet with pink silk. A fringe is knotted on to each end of the antimacassar.

101.—PHOTOGRAPH-STAND.

102.—TABLE-COVER.

No. 85. Table-Cover. (Crewel Stitch.) Table-cover of olive plush with a stripe of claret plush 7 inches wide round the edge at about 3 inches from the fringe. Lines of embroidery and separate flower-patterns are worked upon the claret plush. The upper border is embroidered upon a foundation of holland in crewel stitch. The flowers are worked alternately with blue and white or pink and white silk with dark red centre in knotted stitch; the leaves are worked with olive and yellow silk, and afterwards lined in chain stitch. The holland is then wet with solution of gum-arabic, and when dry the flowers are cut along the outline and sewn on to the plush with chain stitch of yellow silk. The outer part of the flowers is worked with blue and the inner with white silk; the ribs are overcast with silver thread, the inner calices with dark olive, and the outer with yellow silk. The separate flowers should be worked upon the red plush. These are also worked first upon holland in crewel. The colours used are several shades of copper and olive-green. The large convolvulus is embroidered with several shades of bronze; the small flower with blue, and the leaves

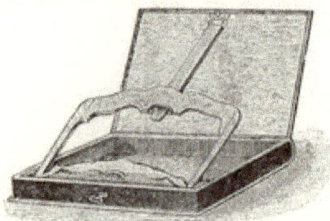

103.—Embroidered Reading-Desk (Open).

104.—Chairback. For Details see Nos. 113 and 114.

106.—Basket Work-Stand. For Detail see No. 97.

105.—Reading-Desk (Shut).

with olive silk. It is then cut out and sewn on to the plush with chain stitching of yellow silk. The cover is lined with claret satin and edged with a fringe of the colours used in the embroidery.

Nos. 86 and 89. Tapestry Mat worked upon dark red cloth with gold crewels and black silk. The pattern—a portion of which we give in the original size in No. 86—is very easy to execute, and most effective when finished.

No. 88. Embroidered Band for a Window-Drapery or Portière. The curtain should consist of old-gold cloth, velvet, or satin, and the band of ruby plush worked with coloured

107.—EMBROIDERED CHAIR.

108.—ALMANACK.

109.—EMBROIDERY FOR ALMANACK.

110.—EMBROIDERY FOR ALMANACK.

silks in any suitable design. The deep valance at the top is of ruby plush and worked like the band of the curtain. Old-gold thick silk cord with grenat and gold tassels loop back the curtain at the sides. A deep old-gold fringe trims the edge of the curtains and valance; this fringe has a grenat heading of silk braid twisted into some fanciful design, which also binds the edges of the embroidered band.

Nos. 87 and 90. Mat. (Embroidery.) Square mat of white silk gauze, embroidered from the design of which we give a fourth part in No. 87. Trace the pattern on the silk, and work the interlaced bars in crewel stitch with light and dark brown silk, working the separate

111.—Embroidery for Tapestry Mat No. 91.

stitches with gold thread. The flowers are all worked in chain stitch with several shades of blue silk, and centre knotted stitch of gold thread. The grass, leaves, and stems are worked with reseda silk in crewel and overcast stitch and in point russe. The gauze is then turned down and worked in open hem-stitching with blue silk. Round the edge is a border of cream-coloured lace.

Nos. 91 and 111. Tapestry Mat, with a cross in the centre and embroidered flowers. The centre design may be a basket of flowers, a little dog, or anything else the worker chooses. No. 111 shows the surrounding flowers.

No. 92. Sofa-Cushion. (Crewel and Overcast Stitch.) Square cushion of olive plush with diagonal stripe of gold satin, embroidered from a South Kensington design. The jasmine flowers and buds are worked with bronze, and the leaves with olive silk in crewel and overcast stitch, the knotted stitch being put in with gold silk. A silk braid is sewn

112.—EMBROIDERY FOR No. 104.

down each side of the embroidery, and the cushion is finished off at the corners with tassels, pompons, and passementerie as shown in the illustration.

Nos. 93 and 94. Chairback. (Embroidery in Satin Stitch.) Chairback of rough Turkish cloth, 40 inches long by 24 wide. The narrow edges are hemmed an inch deep. Above the hem is an embroidery of which No. 94 gives half the design. The pattern is traced on to the ground, and worked with two shades of blue embroidery cotton in chain, overcast, crewel, knotted, and feather stitch, as well as in point russe. The narrow border is worked with the

same cotton in chain and crewel stitch. At each end is a crocheted insertion, and at the lower
edge of the hem a crocheted lace edging.

No. 95. Toilet-Cushion. (Embroidery.) Square cushion covered with dark red plush,
over half of which is placed a triangular part of brocaded olive damask. The separate patterns

113.—TOILET-CUSHION. FOR DETAIL SEE No. 117.

114.—DETAIL OF No. 103.

115.—FOOT-REST. (Embroidery).

of the brocade are edged with braid woven with coloured silk and gold or silver thread,
and filled up in chain stitch and point russe with coloured silks and gold thread. The flowers
are worked with dark and light pink silks, the stems, leaves, and sprays with different shades
of olive-green. The narrow scallops round this part of the work are worked in chain stitch
with bronze silk, and edged with an olive-green braid woven in loops and with the same
braid as that mentioned above. Along the triangle where it meets the plush the two braids are

sewn on in a Greek border, and the cushion is finished off round the edge with a cord of dark red and old-gold silk and with balls of the same colours.

No. 96. This design, which consists of grapes, leaves, and tendrils, may be worked upon silk, satin, cloth, plush, or velvet in black, dark red, dark blue, or brown. The vine-leaves are in two or three shades of rather light green with darker veinings, the grapes and tendrils are in pale green with a darker outline, and may be executed in crewels or silks or both.

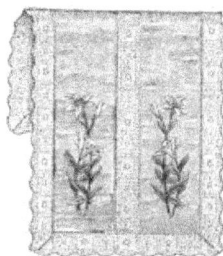

116.—EMBROIDERED CHAIRBACK.

117.—EMBROIDERY FOR No. 113.

Nos. 97 and 106. Basket Workstand. The stand is of willow, fitted with two willow straw baskets, varnished brown and yellow. The upper basket, which has a lid, is ornamented with lambrequins of red cloth, which are embroidered from No. 97 (the original size) in crewel, buttonhole, feather, and chain stitch with thick Oriental wool in pale colours. The flower is worked in pink and blue wool of several shades, the pink leaves being outlined with gold soutache and spangles. The lance-shaped leaves are worked in tea-green wool with feather stitchings of red silk. The smallest leaf is worked with this last-named silk only. The branching stems are worked in shaded blue wool. The round dots are formed of gold soutache in spirals, the connecting stems being in chain stitch of blue silk; the spangles are sewn on with yellow silk. The edging of each lambrequin is a tea-green woollen braid, which is also edged with a narrow gold braid, and a yellow bead galloon sewn on with cross stitches of blue and white silk. The joining of the lambrequins to the basket is concealed by a looped braid of pink, blue, and brown moss wool. At the edge of the lambrequins there is a similar braid, and tassels of tea-green and pink wool at every point. Inside the upper basket is lined with red satin, being first wadded and then tufted with buttons of the same colour. The inside of the lid is lined in the same manner. The edges of the lining are hidden by looped braid. The sides of the basket are of pleated satin, ruched at the top. The bottom of the lower basket is covered with cloth, embroidered like the lambrequins. The insides are lined with pleated red satin, turned back at the top to form a heading. The upper edge of the

118.—GARDEN FURNITURE. FOR DETAIL SEE No. 133.

basket, and also the handle, is ornamented with tea-green and red wool, which is twisted round them. Tassels are hung upon every available point.

No. 98. Embroidered Prayer-book Cover. This design is embroidered on dark velvet with gold cantille, fine gold, thread, and silk. First draw the design on cartoon-paper, cut it out and stitch it on to the velvet, then work it over in crewel and stem stitch. Brush over the wrong side with thick gum-arabic and stick it on the book.

No. 99. Case for Letter-Paper. This case is of wood, and covered with bronze-brown plush, with a small embroidered oval in the centre of the front.

No. 100. Table with Embroidered Cover. Table of light oak, carved in Renaissance style. It has a cover of bronze plush cut exactly to fit the table. It is lined with strong calico and old-gold satine. Previous to the lining the plush is embroidered after the design illustrated, in crewels with floss silk—pink, blue, olive, and red. This is for the flowers and stalks. The centre of each flower is worked in knotted stitch with the darkest shade of colour corresponding to the flower. The stalks and tendrils are worked in loose stem stitch and over-sewn with fine gold thread. The same

thread marks the ribs and veinings of the flowers and leaves. The whole design is then outlined with gold cord sewn on with fine yellow silk. Round the edge of the cover is a knotted
fringe of bronze wool, silk, and gold wire.

No. 101. Embroidered Photograph-Stand. The stand is covered with dark red velvet,
and worked with crewel silks in white pink, pale green, and gold. The ebony frame should
be twisted round with gold cord, and finished off at each corner with some metal *motif.*

No. 102. Worked Table-Cover. Cover of olive silk serge with embroidery at both ends.
After tracing the design on the material work the flowers with maize, yellow, and old-gold silk
in crewel stitch, the leaves and buds in pale and dark olive crewel wool, the stalks in both
shades of the same wool intertwisted. The border is worked in stem stitch and the dots in

119.—Work-Basket.

121.—Pompadour Bag.

120.—Dust-Brush Holder.

satin stitch, and the waved line in outline stitch, also with olive wools. The ends are ornamented
with a netted fringe of olive wool, with balls and tassels of maize, yellow, old-gold, and olive wool.

Nos. 103 and 105. Embroidered Reading-Desk. This reading-desk (of which we give
two designs showing it open and shut) is of wood in the shape of an album. The inside is
polished and the outside covered with red-brown plush with an embroidered design on the lid.
After tracing the design from No. 105, embroider it with coloured crewel silk and crewel and
stem stitch, outlining the design with gold cord. No. 103 shows it open, and No. 105 shut.

Nos. 104, 112, and 114. Embroidered Chairback. For the chairback take a piece of
blue satin 25 inches long and 11 inches wide. At each end cut off 3 inches of the satin and
insert a piece of imitation guipure measuring 3 inches wide. This is sewn on to the satin
with feather stitching; the satin is then worked from the design given in No. 112 in crewel

and stem stitch with split filoselle. No. 114 gives the small design for the border. The water-lily and buds of No. 112 are worked in white, silver-grey, and pale pink silk, the leaves, stalks, and calyx of the bud in olive and brown silk of several shades; the veinings of the leaves should be marked in stem stitch with silk of a darker shade. The design for the border may be worked in pink or white, with leaves and stalks of olive-green. The chair-back is edged with imitation guipure.

No. 107. Embroidered Chair. Chair of polished brown wood, cushioned and covered with dark olive velvet, tufted and fastened with pale yellow buttons. The arms are similarly cushioned. The back and seat are covered with an embroidered Afghan of a finer kind of olive velvet. The lighter leaf designs are cut out of gold satin, the overlying leaves of the large flowers are of claret colour, and the underpart of grey velvet, the side flowers of peacock-blue velvet and pink satin, the calices and the short side leaves of olive velvet. These are all *applied* and

127.—EMBROIDERY FOR GARDEN FURNITURE No. 118.

surrounded with warm-coloured silk cord. The lighter parts of the design are outlined with a darker cord. Small flowers and leaves are embroidered in crewel silks on various parts of the appliqué-work in crewel, knotted, and stem stitch in the various colours of the appliqués. The arabesques are formed of two rows of gold cord connected by long cross stitches of olive silk. The Afghan should be lined with some contrasting colour of cashmere or merino, and finish at each end with a gimp-headed fringe of wool and silk combining all the colours of the embroidery.

Nos. 108, 109, and 110. Almanack with Embroidered Frame. The frame is made of thick cardboard covered with embroidered plush (olive). The design for the embroidery is taken from No. 110; it is traced on the material and then worked in crewel, knotted, and basket stitch. The flower at the corner is worked in heliotrope silk; the 5-petalled flowers are worked in several shades of blue silk, the leaves with olive, and the branching stems in brown floss silk. The figures are then outlined with fine gold cord, sewn on with yellow silk. Another design for the same frame may be taken from No. 109. The design is traced on coloured velvet, the edelweiss is formed of white chenille with a cream centre worked in crewel stitch, crossed with small brown silk stitches. The forget-me-nots are worked in satin stitch with blue silk, and white centres in knotted stitch. The stems and leaves are worked in crewel and stem stitch with olive silk.

Nos. 113 and 117. Embroidered Toilet-Cushion. The cushion itself is covered with four pieces of copper-coloured plush arranged in the form of a Maltese cross. Between the arms of the cross pieces of pleated old-gold satin may be seen. The plush is embroidered from No. 117 in crewel or satin stitch. The flowers and buds are worked in pink or blue, with yellow centres in satin stitch, and knotted stitch in olive. Veinings of fine gold silk. The stalks and leaves are worked in several shades of olive. In the middle of the cushion there is a knot of olive plush embroidered with old-gold silk in point russe. It is surrounded with a narrow pleating of old-gold satin. The under-side of the cushion is covered with the same material. A brass button is sewn on at each corner to form feet for the cushion.

113.—EMBROIDERY FOR A WHATNOT.

No. 115. Embroidered Foot-Rest. An oblong cushion, with a centre of olive velvet, worked in crewels. Trace the design on white calico; cut it out and place it on the velvet, then worked over the calico in crewels. The inner leaves of the large flower are in blue satin stitch, and the outer with crosswise stitches of pale pink silk, with points of a darker pink. The upper part of this flower is worked in 4 shades of pink, the buds worked in the same manner with pink, blue, and olive. The leaves, which are worked with brownish and olive silks, have an overlying leaf worked in dark red silk. Each figure is outlined with gold cord, sewn on with fine yellow silk. The long branching leaves are worked in crewel stitch with brown shaded silk and Smyrna stitch in gold thread. The cushion is covered with puffed olive satin, fastened down with olive buttons. The setting-on of the embroidered centre is hidden by a gimp of olive wool and silk, with small woollen balls at intervals. A second plain gimp, with a deep ball fringe, finishes the cushion. Wooden handles, covered with floss silk and cord, serve to lift the cushions.

No. 116. Embroidered Chairback. For this chairback take a piece of old-gold satin measuring 12 inches broad by 25 long. Down the middle is a strip of imitation guipure insertion;

the satin is cut away from beneath. The chairback is then embroidered in the design shown in illustration. After tracing it on the satin work the flowers in white filoselle, the leaves and stalks in several shades of olive in crewel and stem stitch. Finish the chairback with an edging of guipure lace.

Nos. 118 and 122. Garden Furniture. This pretty garden suite comprises chairs, circular table, and small footstool, all of cane, worked in a mosaic pattern. Illustration 122 gives the design for the antimacassar thrown over one of the lounge-chairs. The pattern is embroidered on a ground of écru-coloured Java canvas in strips, worked partly in crewel, chain stitch, and

114.—CENTREPIECE OF EMBROIDERY FOR A WHATNOT.

point russe, and partly in a plaited stitch of brown wool interspersed with an open-work design. It consists of a cross seam and a double row of plaited stitch, with open-work between. Beginning from the middle of the strip, pass over 7 threads and work the narrow way a row of plaited stitch as follows:—° Pass the thread slantwise from left to right over 6 threads high and 2 broad, and then back from right to left over 4 threads high and 2 broad; repeat from °. Miss 5 threads of canvas, and work another row of plaited stitch. Two similar rows are worked up the second half of the centre strip. Then proceed for the open-work pattern as follows:—For the centre pattern leave the 4 centre threads unnoticed and draw out 4 threads lengthwise on either side, so that there is only 1 strand left. With the horizontal threads a cross seam must be worked with brown wool in the centre 4 threads, taking 4 crossway threads on the right side and 4 canvas threads on the wrong. Between the rows of plaited stitch pull out 3 vertical threads of canvas. The pattern is worked on the horizontal threads, so that the 4 threads cross. To do this pass the écru-coloured thread under the 4th and 3rd threads, taking in the 1st and 2nd threads, and bringing them to the outside. The next 34 threads are embroidered according to the pattern given in Illustration 122, which is worked in crewels or silks in satin and chain stitch and point russe. The narrow strips are embroidered in the centre to correspond with the one above described, and edged on each side as follows :—Work a row of buttonhole stitch over 4 threads broad and 2 high, turn the work, and work another row back again, taking in the first row as the illustration shows.

No. 119. Embroidered Work-Basket. This basket is of polished reeds and straw braid. The middle is ornamented with a strip of coloured stamped cloth, which is embroidered with crewel silks of several shades of bronze and pink in point russe, stem stitch, and feather stitch. The stamped designs upon the cloth are outlined with twisted braid. The edge of the strip is ornamented with looped braid (bronze), sewn on with point russe stitches of bronze silks. The same braid forms a diagonal pattern across the strip, the loops meeting in the centre. This also is sewn on with point russe stitches. The handles of the basket are ornamented with a crochet chain of dark olive wool, with balls of the same at the edge. Each end of the basket is also ornamented with balls of dark olive and bronze wool, connected by a crochet chain tied in the middle with three woollen tassels to finish it.

No. 120. Dust-Brush Holder. This holder is a sort of basket of reed and willow straw, with a bag of olive velvet sewn in even folds into the bottom of the basket. The folds are drawn closely together at the edge, and finished with a tassel of coloured wool, silk, and gold wire. The front of the basket is covered with a piece of embroidered bronze velvet scalloped at one side. After tracing the design on this velvet, work the centre of the large flower in feather stitch with pale blue, the petals with dark blue silk in crewel stitch, the calyx and stems with pale and dark olive silk. The leaves, flowers, and buds are worked in bronze pink and blue silks, in feather and crewel stitch. The setting-on of the velvet to the basket is hidden by means of balls of coloured wool, silk, and gold wire. The inside of the top has another row of these balls, and where the rings to hang it are fixed there is a very large ball tassel of the same materials. A bow of bronze satin ribbon is sewn to the back.

No. 121. Pompadour Bag. Embroidered Bag of bronze plush lined with satin of the same colour and worked in crewels. Lay the plush and satin together and cut them together to form a piece 6 inches by 21. This piece will make the bottom of the bag. For the upper portion cut a piece measuring 9 inches by 12. Round off the corners of this last, and work the embroidery for the upper piece in crewel silk and cord (old gold). For the branches and stems use darker gold cord. Then join the plush and satin together, round off the lower corners of the embroidered part, join it to the lower piece which has been previously gathered (as shown in the illustration). Next gather the top twice, about an inch from the edge, inserting a piece of elastic between the two gatherings so as to draw up the bag. Add double dark bronze cords on each side, and make a knot of the same in the lower portion of the bag to form a tassel.

Nos. 123 and 124. The design which we give for a whatnot is embroidered in satin stitch with

G

crewels on Java canvas. It is very easy to work, and very beautiful when finished. Our illustrations show the sidepiece and the bouquet of the centre in full size. This bouquet consists of field-flowers and ears of corn, which are all worked in their different colours. The petals of the daisies are worked with white crewels and covered with white silk, the heart with yellow silk in knotted stitch. The ears of corn are worked in lilac, the cornflowers in blue, with black stamens, each of which is surmounted with a knotted stitch in white silk. The large petals of the poppies are worked in close crewel stitch. Work the stitch short, and make several rows, changing the tints from the shades marked on the illustration. The stitch of one row must come between those of another, so as to fill the space entirely. The heart is worked in green wool, the stamens last of all, with black silk tipped with a knotted stitch. The ears of corn are worked in two shades of yellow, the foliage in different shades of green wool. The veinings are worked last of all, and must be embroidered in some colour forming a good contrast. The stems are olive-green and dark and light wood colour in overcast. The whatnot is not difficult to mount. Stretch the canvas on cardboard lined on both sides with silk or satin; bend the front part so as to give it a round shape, and sew it against the back; the seams must be covered with chenille. The whatnot is completed with cords, tassels, and bows in passementerie.

CHAPTER IX.

DESCRIPTION OF FOLDED SUPPLEMENTS.

No. 1.—*Sheet of Crewel Designs.*

WE will begin with the plastron of wild flowers, which consists of buttercups, daisies, rye-grass, and forget-me-nots.

The design should be worked upon black or white satin. The buttercups in gold silk with green stalks and leaves, the daisies in white, with pink edges and yellow centres, the rye-grass in bright green, and the forget-me-nots in blue, with yellow centres and green leaves. Carefully executed with regard to colour, this design is pretty and effective.

The next is the pretty little cuff for a dress, which is worked in violets and leaves. These violets should not all be worked in the same colour. The two at the top might be white, with a *soupçon* of pink at the stalk, the two large ones at the side in mauve, and the rest in purple. The leaves and stalks are green; the latter should not be quite so dark as the former.

We also give a little pocket and collar of the same design—viz., violets and leaves.

A pretty embroidered collar is the one with a design of briony and leaves. The flower is pale lemon colour, the leaves green, with the veinings shaded so as to give them the appearance of being raised (see illustration).

The Mazarin collar, or dress yoke, has a design of marsh-mallows and leaves. The flower is a deeper yellow than a buttercup, and the leaves are a medium shade of green.

Next on our list comes the bodice for a pinafore costume. The design consists of green ivy with oak veinings and tendrils.

The jessamine for a parasol-cover is white, with green cups and leaves, and a pale brown stalk. Two pretty little corners, one of lilies of the valley, another of moss-rosebuds, will be found useful for various purposes.

All these designs may be adapted to other articles of dress or furniture. For instance, the forget-me-nots are suitable for embroidering a tea-cosy or the edge of a five-o'clock tea-cloth, with a small bunch of the same in the centre.

The marsh-mallow would be effective as a trimming for the edge of curtains or a portière, while the violets would embroider the front of a dress or jacket. The ivy might be used for any of the purposes above mentioned, while the little corners would be suitable for a hand-kerchief-basket or cigar-case. The marsh-mallows would also be effective for embroidering a sofa-cushion or antimacassar.

No. 2.—*"Alice in Wonderland" Tea-cloth.*

This design is for a Five o'Clock Tea-cloth. The drawings are enlarged from those of Mr. John Tenniel in that most charming of children's books, "Alice's Adventures in Wonderland," the author, Mr. Lewis Carroll, having kindly given us permission to reproduce them. We also owe our acknowledgments to the publishers, Messrs. Macmillan. "The Mad Tea Party" forms our largest and central picture. This delightful tea party is now universally known wherever the English language is spoken. As a proof that this is no exaggerated statement, we may mention the fact that a dramatised version of the book was acted some years ago at an Indian station by the officers of the Fifth Lancers, one of whom achieved a tremendous success in the *rôle* of the caterpillar, in which his writhings were marvellous. For the benefit of the unfortunate few who have not read the book, we may remark that the tea party consisted of the hatter, the March-hare, and the dormouse, the latter of whom was in a chronic state of sleep, like the fat boy in Dickens's "Pickwick." Alice joins them, and is much astonished and disgusted at the extreme rudeness of their manners and the unanswerable character of their riddles. There is surely no possible answer to such a riddle as, "Why is a raven like a writing-desk?" Alice at last leaves them, and as she is trotting off in a pet looks back and sees the hatter and the March-hare trying to put the dormouse into the teapot, an incident the illustration of which occupies one of the corners of our tea-cloth. Another of our corner pictures shows Alice after she had eaten the cake, and had in consequence shrunk to so small a size that the little puppy was a gigantic creature as compared with her.

"Hardly knowing what she did, she picked up a little bit of stick, and held it out to the puppy; where-upon the puppy jumped into the air off all its feet at once, with a yelp of delight, and rushed at the stick, and made believe to worry it; then Alice dodged behind a great thistle, to keep herself from being run over, and the moment she appeared on the other side the puppy made another rush at the stick, and tumbled head over heels in its hurry to get hold of it. Then Alice, thinking it was very like having a game of play with a cart-horse, and expecting every moment to be trampled under its feet, ran round the thistle again. Then the puppy began a series of short charges at the stick, running a very little way forwards each time and a long way back, till at last it sat down a good way off, panting, with its tongue hanging out of its mouth, and its great eyes half-shut."

Alice escapes after this episode, which by the way shows an intimate acquaintance with the delightful ways of dogs on the part of the author, and finds herself near a large mushroom, and on peeping over the edge of it finds that a large blue caterpillar is sitting on the top smoking a long hookah. This incident is also illustrated in a corner of our Five-o'Clock Tea-cloth. For their amusing interview we must refer our readers to the book itself; but we cannot resist the temptation of transcribing part of the parody on Southey's "You are hale, Father William."

"You are old, Father William," the young man said,
"And your hair has become very white;
And yet you incessantly stand on your head—
Do you think, at your age, it is right?"

"In my youth," Father William replied to his son,
"I feared it might injure the brain;
But now that I'm perfectly sure I have none,
Why, I do it again and again."

"You are old," said the youth, "as I mentioned before,
And have grown most uncommonly fat;
Yet you turned a back somersault in at the door—
Pray, what is the reason of that?"

"In my youth," said the sage, as he shook his grey locks,
"I kept all my limbs very supple
By the use of this ointment—one shilling the box—
Allow me to sell you a couple?"

"You are old," said the youth, "and your jaws are too weak
For anything tougher than suet;
Yet you finished the goose, with the bones and the beak—
Pray, how do you manage to do it?"

"In my youth," said his father, "I took to the law,
And argued each case with my wife,
And the muscular strength which it gave to my jaw
Has lasted the rest of my life."

One of our illustrations shows the Lobster's Quadrille, the performers in the present instance being the Mock Turtle, the Gryphon, and Alice herself. The tea-cloth looks remarkably well worked on yellow crash or linen with brown wool or silk.

No. 3.—*Embroidery for Jacket or Dress.*

This sheet represents an embroidered tight summer jacket, cut to fit a figure measuring 26 inches round the waist, and 36 round the bust. It can be cut from two yards of 54-inch cloth. The shape is quite tight-fitting. The pattern is equal, for all intents and purposes, to a cut-out one, as each section of the jacket is clearly outlined and ready for cutting. The letters that appear upon each portion of the design indicate where each is to be joined to the other. A is joined to A; B to B; and so on.

Our embroidery design consists of the blossom and leaves of the harebell. It is not difficult to work, being a flower with such slight stem and leaves. The colours in which it should be worked are white and sage green, inclining to bronze or brown. The white should have a creamy tint, not pure white. The extreme delicacy and transparency of the natural flower can thus be indicated, whereas if a pure, snowdrop white were used, the blossom would look too thick. Two tints of brownish green will suffice for the leaves, the darker one to be used for the stalks. The design can be utilised for a child's dress, or a polonaise for a grown-up person. The best mode of transferring it to the material is by means of Mr. Francis' Transferring Apparatus, costing 2s. 6d. This is so simple that the least intelligent person could manage it, provided the necessary precaution be taken of having a very hard surface upon which to draw— glass is the best. We give a very pretty collar and cuff. The deeper part of the collar is the front. In making it up it should be lined with silk. This jacket is suitable for being made in similar material to that of the dress.

DESCRIPTION OF COLOURED SUPPLEMENT.

This pretty coloured design is intended to be worked in crewels, and consists of cornflowers, poppies, wheat, and daisies. The colours required are two shades of blue for the cornflowers, one very pale, the other a rich shade of ultramarine, two shades of red for the poppies, two of yellow for the ox-eyed wheat, four shades of green (two of blue-green and two of sage-green), two shades of white for the daisies, and two shades of greenish brown for the shading of the leaves. The design is not a difficult one to work, and may be executed upon satin, velvet, or plush in silks or crewels. A five o'clock tea-cloth worked with it would be pretty and appropriate, also a cosey, sofa-cushion, chair-back, music-stool, footstool, mat, &c. The worker should be careful in choosing her blue-green not to have it too vivid, and the greenish brown should be more inclined to green than brown. The two reds will not be difficult to choose, and those who have the opportunity will do well to match the colours from the tints of the natural flowers.

The colour of the foundation, be it silk, satin, plush, or velvet, should be either black, dark green, dark blue, old gold, or grey. We should not recommend either red or brown.

DESIGN FOR FIVE O'CLOCK TEA CLOTH

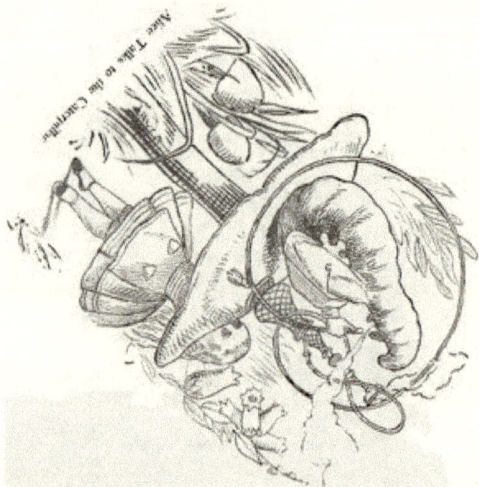

After Talks in the Cuckoo.

CLOTH AND EMBROIDERED DRESS TRIMMING

Putting the Dormouse in the Teapot.

The Lobsters' Quadrille

From Side-piece

FULL-SIZED PATTERN

OF

A SUMMER JACKET.

WITH

ARTISTIC DESIGN FOR EMBROIDERY

IN OUTLINE STITCH OR CREWEL.